Cathar Country

An independent holiday guide to

CARCASSONNE

and

the *département* of AUDE

Revised 2nd Edition

Trevor Park

© 2014 Trevor Park ISBN 978-0-9508325-5-5
St Bega Publications

Welcome to Carcassonne
and the *département* of Aude

This independent holiday guide offers a wealth of choice of places to see and things to do for people of all ages and tastes. It is divided into short, easy-to-manage sections arranged thematically for ease of reference. It will help your advance planning in a big way whilst being light enough not to weigh down your luggage. The 1st edition was very well received by travellers to the region as the many five star reviews published on Amazon testify. I hope this revised 2nd edition will prove to be equally helpful.

When you come, you will quickly discover what an area of outstanding natural beauty Aude is and what a wealth of history it has for you to explore and enjoy. The county town of Carcassonne has just over 47,000 inhabitants but it is reckoned to be second only to Paris in the number of visitors it attracts. About three million people come here each year and most of them come in the summer. At times it can get very crowded in the *Cité* which is the top attraction. With the additional publicity it has been given by Kate Mosse's best selling novels *Labyrinth*, *Sepulchre* and *Citadel* the number of visitors from the UK has risen, helped too by the low-cost airline Ryanair which now flies over 300,000 passengers a year from Dublin, Bournemouth, the East Midlands, Liverpool and Stansted.

My family had been coming on holiday to this area for many years before we bought a home near Carcassonne twelve years ago. We have visited all the tourist sites described in this guide, some of them many times, so I can recommend them with confidence. I have given details of their websites where these exist so that you can find out more about the particular places or activities which are of special interest to you. It also allows you to check out opening times and admission charges in the month you will be visiting, and to get the latest information about what's on when you will be here. The centre page is a map of the *département* published by the Aude Tourist Board and I have provided a grid reference on this map for every site described in the book.

One consequence of the decline in the local wine industry is that much more attention is now being given to tourism. Even small villages are now laying on cultural events and entertainment which will be of interest to visitors and they are publicising these attractions more effectively. It is worth calling in at the village tourist information offices to find out what is going on locally whilst you are down here. If you can come in the spring or later in the autumn when it is still warm and sunny, you will find the *Cité* and the beaches far less crowded.

Bonnes vacances! Enjoy your holiday.   **Trevor Park**

Contents

Acknowledgements: Thanks to the Aude Tourist Board for permission to use the map on pages 30-31 and to the Carcassonne Tourist Board for permission to use the maps on page 7 and on the back cover. Thanks also to Alan Reynolds for the 6 sketch maps on pages 46-50, and to Tim Mitchley for pictures of the *Cité* and of the castles. And lastly to Sunniva Park for her help in compiling and checking the Practical Information.

All information was correct when this Guide was printed but opening times and admission fees etc may have changed since then. Do check the websites for the latest information.

Carcassonne - *La Cité*

A tingle of excited anticipation may well be your immediate reaction on first seeing the *Cité*. For this is the best restored medieval walled city in Europe. UNESCO designated it a World Heritage Site in 1997. Standing high above the River Aude and with its twin concentric walls and 52 towers, its drawbridges and inner castle, it is the realisation of every child's dream of what a fortified city looks like. When you walk along its crowded, narrow streets or sit by the moat outside the *Château Comtal*, it's not hard to imagine yourself back in the 13th century. Come in July or August and you can watch actors dressed as medieval knights jousting in the *lices*, the grassy area between the outer and inner walls. And there are plenty of shops where plastic or wooden swords and shields can be bought, and space enough in the *lices* or along the ramparts where children (and adults) can live out their fantasy of being a knight, defending the city against the northern invaders in 1209. For a fortnight in mid-August there is a medieval festival at which part of the history of the city is re-enacted, and there is plenty of street entertainment with jugglers, and fire-eaters and musicians. If you are here on Bastille Day, July 14th, you can watch *L'embrasement de la Cité*, a spectacular firework display. Despite not starting until 22.30 and lasting just half an hour, vast crowds of spectators come to see it. It is as though the entire *Cité* were ablaze.

There has been a fortified settlement here since the 6th century BC. It was held first by the Gauls, then by the Romans, followed by the Visigoths, Saracens and Franks. Its golden age was from 1089-1209 when the Trencavels, who were also Viscounts of Béziers and Nimes, were its rulers. Like many other tolerant, southern noble families they allowed Jews and adherents of the Cathar faith to live in their cities. The Cathars or *Bon Hommes* who saw themselves as the true heirs of Christ posed a serious challenge to the dominant and decadent Roman Catholic Church. In 1208 following the killing of a Papal Legate, Pope Innocent III called for a crusade against these heretics. At this time the region in the deep south was not part of France and it was an army of northern knights who waged war with the blessing not just of the Pope but also of the French King who saw it as an opportunity to extend the borders of his kingdom. The *Cité* fell to the crusaders after a short siege in the summer of 1209 and on the death of Raymond Roger Trencavel later that year a northern baron, Simon de Montfort, was declared Viscount. He took over the Trencavel lands as well as command of the invading army. The war dragged on for years with some extremely savage episodes in it. De Montfort was killed at the siege of Toulouse in 1218. The end came in 1244 with the fall of Montsegur Castle and the burning alive of the 144 Cathars captured there who refused to give up their faith.

Before entering the *Cité* by the *Porte Narbonaise* which was built about 1280, it's worth taking a ride either in the small tourist train (adults 7€ children 3€) or in a *caleche*, a horse-drawn carriage along the *lices* to see just how extensive the walls are. Later you can walk along part of the ramparts. Once you have passed over the drawbridge and through the barbican, head up the lane to the Count's castle, a perfect example of medieval military architecture. There are guided tours usually on the hour or you can explore it on your own. The castle is open from 09.30-18.30 April – September, and 09.30-17 the rest of the year (admission: adults 8.50€).

A short walk down Rue Saint Louis is the Basilica of St Nazaire, begun in 1096 in Romanesque style by the Trencavals and completed in Gothic style two hundred years later by the King of France. It has two singularly beautiful rose windows from the 13th and 14th centuries in the north and south transepts. There is more 13th century stained glass in two of the chapels. The organ which dates from 1522 is the finest in the south of France and free recitals are given at 17.00 every Sunday from mid-June to mid-September. Not far from the cathedral is the *Porte d'Aude* pictured below. It is certainly worth walking through and going a short way down the hill to appreciate what a marvellous defence it was.

When you are ready to eat, the *Place Marcou* is ringed by *brasseries* and restaurants with many more in the streets nearby. You can spend an enjoyable half hour simply browsing menus and comparing prices which are always displayed outside the restaurant. Inevitably the quality is variable, so check to see if there are any recommendations listed such as Routard or Michelin.

Afterwards, there are several shops worth a look inside, selling lace and tapestry work, linen goods, wooden toys, locally made sweets, regional delicacies, and the wares of potters and wood turners and metalworkers but many of the shops are simply outlets for picture postcards and souvenirs, soft drinks and ices. There are a few small museums. The *Musée de l'Ecole* at 3 *rue de Plo* is about school life in the late 19th and early 20th century and can be of interest for young and old alike (see page 22).

Despite the crowds of tourists in summer, the *Cité* is a wonderful place to visit. Reckon on spending half a day or longer in it. Arrive early morning and you

will avoid the crowds. It is just about accessible for wheelchairs but difficult, especially as you go through the Narbonne Gate.

You can enjoy a virtual tour of the *Cité* at www. carcassonne-culture. fr and you can find out more at www.tourisme-carcassonne.fr

Carcassonne – *La Bastide* the lower City

The shuttle bus (*navette*) will take you from the Narbonne Gate down to the lower city stopping outside the railway station which is by the *Canal du Midi* and the *André Chénier* Gardens – see the Town Map B1 on the next page. If you prefer to walk, exit by the Aude Gate and go down the hill over the 14th century *Pont Vieux* heading for the walls of the *Bastide* St Louis, the city built on the orders of King Louis in 1247 after he had annexed the region. If you are driving, follow the signs for *centre ville*. There are underground car parks at Square Gambetta, by the *André Cheniér* Gardens and under *Place du General de Gaulle*. There is plenty of parking along *Boulevard Barbès* which is free during the lunch hours of 12 – 14.

The heart of the *bastide* which is built to a draught board layout is the *Place Carnot* – Town Map B2. Its centrepiece is a large, baroque fountain depicting Neptune built by an Italian sculptor in the 18th century. The base of the fountain as well as the pavements around the square are laid with the distinctive red marble from Caunes Minervois. A market is held in the square on Tuesdays, Thursdays and Saturdays in the morning. It is especially good on Saturdays - stalls piled high with fresh, local, seasonal produce: peaches, melons, olives, nuts, asparagus, all kinds of vegetables, flowers, home-made bread, honey, cheeses, and much else. Nearby is *les Halles,* the indoor market which has 18 large stalls selling fresh fish, meat, poultry and cheeses.

There are 8 *café-bars* and *brasseries* around the square, and their tables and sunshades cover the square in summer. In the surrounding streets you will find a number of small restaurants where you can enjoy a three course set lunch for 15-20 euros; try *L'Als'Assiette* on *Rue Armagnac* or *L'Endroit* on *rue de l'Aigle d'Or*. If you don't want a full meal there are *patisseries* selling mouth-watering pastries and cakes, and take-away pizza places and pancake shops where you can also buy soft drinks.

There is a good range of shops including some elegant clothes boutiques and a very fine, old-style grocer's *La Ferme* at 55 *rue de Verdun* which is one of the main shopping streets. Another is the pedestrianized *rue Georges Clemenceau* which runs from the square up to the station, and the *rue Barbès*. If you need an internet café there is one at 5 *rue Courtjaire* Town Map B2

Outside estate agents, of which there are many, you can pick up free copies of their monthly magazines listing properties for sale, tempting visitors to move down here. Though be warned, the days of buying an old property in need of restoration at a bargain price are almost gone. You might, however, be lucky!

A short walk away from *Place Carnot* is the Cathedral of St Michel Map B2. Built as a parish church in the 13th and 14th centuries, it became the cathedral of the diocese in 1803. Following a fire in 1849 it was renovated by Viollet le Duc, the man responsible for the restoration of the *Cité*. St Vincent's Church on the *rue Armagnac* dating from 1242 is a fine example of Gothic architecture and has the second widest nave in France. There are some fine 18th century private mansions (called '*hôtels*' in French but they are not hotels!); the Museum of Fine Arts is housed in one of them, the Presidial, at 1 *rue de Verdun*. Its permanent collection is mostly of 18th and 19th century French, Dutch and Italian artists and it has a whole room of paintings done by the Carcassonne artist Jacques Gamelin (1738-1803). It also hosts excellent, temporary exhibitions and is occasionally the venue for concerts especially by local musicians. Entry to the museum is free – open 10-17 every day during the summer. In 2012 the *Jardin du Bastion du Calvaire* (planned by a RC priest in 1825) on *Boulevard Barbès* was restored and opened to the public – entrance is free via *rue Voltaire*.

During the summer there are guided tours of the *Cité* and the Lower City starting at 9.30 (Tuesday – Saturday) from the Tourist Office which is at 28 *rue de Verdun*. Audio guides (3€) are available for hire there all year. The city's main tourist website provides a monthly list of every kind of entertainment and activity, including sport. There is, for example, a water jousting tournament in late September and full and half marathons in October.

From May to September, small electric *toucs* transport people around the lower city – they are equipped to take passengers with reduced mobility.

A lovely way to spend a lazy afternoon digesting lunch is to take the short boat trip along the *Canal du Midi* from the harbour by the André Cheniér Gardens. These canal boat trips run from May to November. If you are feeling more energetic, you can hire a bike nearby (12€ for half a day) at 'Generation VTT' based by the port in front of the railway station or from 'Carca'Velo' at 40 rue de Verdun, and then cycle along the old, tree-shaded tow path which runs alongside the canal. Buy a baguette and some cheese and wine and enjoy a picnic in the sunshine by one of the locks, watching the cruisers entering and leaving them. Bliss!

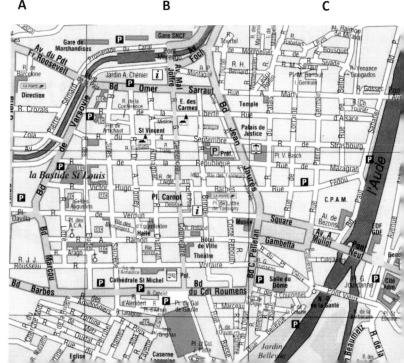

Castles: 'The Sons of Carcassonne'

The Pope launched a crusade in 1209 against the Cathars or *Bon Hommes* living in this region. They were regarded as heretics and a danger to the Catholic Church. Following the capture by the Crusaders of Béziers, Bram, Carcassonne, Lastours, Minerve, and other places harbouring Cathars and the execution of prisoners holding that faith, the survivors found refuge in a number of mountain top castles of which the most famous is Montsegur. The last to hold out was Quéribus which was handed over to the King of France's seneschal in 1255. Five of these castles were known as the 'Sons of Carcassonne': Puilaurens, Termes, Aguilar, Peyrepertuse and Quéribus, all of them situated to the south of Carcassonne and originally meant to protect the borders of the kingdom of Aragon.

They are often incorrectly called 'Cathar Castles'. They were in fact simply castles belonging to local nobles who allowed Cathars to find sanctuary in them. Two in the 'must be seen' category are Quéribus and Peyrepertuse. Fortunately both are situated within sight of each other in the Corbières hills. There is an entrance fee at most of the castles – usually about 5€ for adults and 3€ for children, though some charge a bit more. Opening times vary but in mid-summer most are open from about 10 – 20.

Puilaurens Centre page map C4, stands guardian at a height of 690 metres over the pass that leads towards the upper valley of the Aude. It is a steep climb up a forest track from the car park above the village of Lapradelle-Puilaurens but there are substantial remains to see once you get there, including a keep and some fine crenallated walls. There are magnificent views from the battlements. Find out more at www.puilaurens.com

Aguilar Map E3 is situated on a small hill near Vingrau with fine views over the garrigue. It was originally a Catalan stronghold. It consists of an older, inner pentagonal keep around which octagonal walls were built about the end of the 13th century long after the Crusade against the Cathars.

Termes Map D3 Little remains of this castle whose lord, Raymond de Termes, was a supporter of the Cathars and gave them sanctuary. It was besieged by the northern army in 1210 and the garrison was killed when they tried to flee. A short film is shown in the village museum about the siege. Restoration work is in progress. See www.chateau-termes.com

Quéribus Map D4 pictured above has a spectacular location, balanced on a pinnacle of rock and standing above a sheer cliff. No wonder it was never captured! There are breath taking views from its roof across to the Pyrenees in the south, away to the coast in the east, and inland over vineyards and villages

to Peyrepertuse in the distance on its high, rocky perch. The castle is a 20 minutes walk from the car park and then a steep climb up to the outer walls. Among its several attractions is a fine vaulted Gothic keep. Audio guide tapes are available for hire. www.cucugnan.fr

Peyrepertuse Map D3 is 800 metres up and perched on a long narrow mountain ridge with drops of hundreds of metres on three sides. It makes a most dramatic skyline. On very windy days or during an electrical storm, standing on its walls is no place to be! 300 metres long by 50 wide, it is the largest of all these mountain top sanctuaries; spacious enough to have room for a small village at the lower level plus a chapel built in 1115. The upper part of the castle is an additional fortification built after it became French. Be warned - It is a steep climb from the car park to the castle. You can get a particularly fine view of the castle and the limestone cliff on which it stands from the village of Cucugnan. A four day medieval festival is held here in early August at which the Knights of Peyrepertuse *Les Frères d'Armes* take part in jousting. In the spring and summer there are also displays of falconry. Find out more at www.chateau-peyrepertuse.com

At Montfernier Belvédère near **Lastours** Map C1 there is a look out point which gives a panoramic view across to the four castles pictured above before you descend to the village in the valley of the river Orbiel and then start the steep climb up to them. The remains of the medieval village which was probably deserted about 1240 have been excavated and the finds are now on display in an archaeological exhibition *Lastours, 4000 ans d'histoire.* There is also a gastronomic restaurant there called *Le Puits du Trésors.*

At **Puivert** Map B3 there is a 14th century castle with a keep 35 metres high and a main courtyard. See www.chateau-de-puivert.com There are also the remains of castles at **Saissac** www.saissac.fr Map B1 and **Arques** www.chateau-arques.fr Map C3 where Cathars found refuge during the Crusade. And at **Villerouge Terménès** Map D3 pictured below where Guilhem Bélibaste, the last Cathar *parfait* to be burned at the stake, died in 1321. The castle belonged at that time to the Archbishop of Narbonne though the only time he ever visited it was to watch Bélibaste's execution. There is an audio-visual presentation in

the castle entitled *Le Monde de Guilhem Bélibaste* which is about Catharism and the power of the Catholic Church in the 14th century.

The Aude Tourist Board has a good, free 16 page publication called 'Catharism' which gives a brief account of each castle. See www.payscathare.org

Medieval Abbeys
and Churches

Religion affected every aspect of life in the Middle Ages and the Roman Catholic Church had a monopoly in Western Europe. A chapel or church was to be found in almost every village in this region. The monastic orders were major land-owners and the remains of their abbeys can still be seen. Some of them stand as silent witnesses to a bygone age but others are still in use as parish churches. Here is a selection of the best but you will find that many a village has a medieval church not listed here which is worth seeing. Most abbeys are open from 10 – 19 in the summer but opening times do vary and some close for a two-hour lunch break. Admission charges vary but are about 4€ for adults and 2€ for children.

Several of the major churches have stone carving done by a brilliant 12th century itinerant craftsman whose work is to be seen as far afield as northern Spain and Tuscany in Italy. Sadly his name is not known. He is referred to now as the Master of Cabestany, the name of a small village near Perpignan, in whose church a magnificent timpanum carved by him was discovered in 1930 which provoked international interest in his work. So far 120 sculptures by him have been identified. Examples of his work are to be found at Lagrasse, St Hilaire, St Papoul and Rieux Minervois.

Lagrasse Map D2 is listed among *Les Plus Beaux Villages de France* and deservedly so for its setting, its picturesque, narrow medieval streets and market place, a hump-backed bridge over the River Orbieu dating from the 12th century and its Abbey, which was founded as a Benedictine community in 799, and dedicated to St Mary. See www.lagrasse.com

Caunes-Minervois Map D1 is famous for its red marble quarries and for its abbey church pictured above which was founded in 780. It has a fine crypt open to the public, a 12th century sculpted Norman doorway, cloisters, conventual buildings and a three-storey bell tower. It has a well stocked reception and sales room, and has several small exhibitions of art, marble artefacts, prehistoric pottery found locally and pieces of carved stonework. It hosts a series of classical concerts on Friday evenings during the summer. It serves now as the town's parish church whose clergy are Benedictine monks.

Saint Papoul Map B1 is named after the 4th century evangelist to this area. This imposing, fortified Benedictine abbey was founded in the 8th century. The church dates from the 12th century and the cloisters were rebuilt in the 14th. It is rich in stone carvings done by the Master of Cabestany and there is an exhib-ition of the sculptor's work in the refectory, showing plaster casts and photo-graphs of his work done elsewhere. See www.saint-papoul.fr

Rieux-Minervois Map D1 The village's parish church which dates from the 12th century is architecturally unique in France being seven-sided. Its ambulatory has 14 capitals with some exceptional stone carvings such as the

one of the Assumption of the Blessed Virgin Mary. There is also a striking, multi-coloured 15th century representation of Christ being laid in the tomb.

Saint Hilaire Map C2 is another Benedictine fortified abbey founded in the 8th century. The present church was begun in Romanesque style at the end of the 12th century and has a 13th century Gothic nave with the reliquary of the martyr St. Sernin, the first Bishop of Toulouse, carved in the form of a sarco-phagus from a single block of Pyrenean white marble by the Master of Cabestany. It is a masterpiece! The superb Gothic cloisters pictured below have 54 arches dating from the 14th century. St Hilaire is also the birthplace of the oldest sparkling wine in the world. Blanquette de Limoux was invented by the monks at the abbey in 1531.

The abbey at **Fontfroide** Map E2 pictured above was founded as a Benedictine community in 1093. Following a visit by St Bernard to the Langue-doc in 1145 it became affiliated to the Cistercians and soon became one of that order's greatest abbeys in Europe. After the French Revolution the monastic buildings were confiscated and sold to various landowners but all were preserved. In 1908 Gustave and Madeleine Fayet bought the site in an auction sale and began the work of renovation which is still being done today. Since 1909 it has hosted many painters and musicians and is still a centre for classical music. It has extensive rose gardens with 3,000 rose trees. It also boasts a fine restaurant and there is a picnic area. Visitors can freely walk the land around the abbey but entrance to all the monastic buildings is only permitted as part of a guided tour which costs 10€ for adults and 3.50€ for children under 15. The tour lasts about an hour and the guides speak only French but audio guides in English are provided. See www.fontfroide.com

Villelongue Map B1 near St Papoul has a former Cistercian abbey dating from the 12th century with a cloister from the beginning of the 14th and it has some very pretty gardens. It is now privately owned and is gradually being restored but much remains to be done. Art exhibitions and concerts are held in

the refectory and it hosts an annual scarecrow contest in aid of charities - in 2014 it will be on Sunday 21 September. See www.abbaye-de-villelongue.com

The RC Diocese of Carcassonne and Narbonne has published an excellent illustrated guide to seven Church Trails taking in the best of the medieval ecclesiastical architecture in Aude. The title of the guide is *Balades en Pays d'Aude Itineraires touristiques du patrimonie religieux audeois.*

The Canal du Midi

This is the second UNESCO World Heritage Site in the *département* of Aude. Built between 1666 and 1681 it links the Mediterranean Sea with the Atlantic Ocean. It was built originally to be a mercantile waterway taking the produce of the southern Languedoc region and imports from other Mediterranean lands to the Atlantic for export. It runs from the port of Sète to the city of Toulouse where it meets up with the River Garonne which flows westwards to Bordeaux and the Gironde Estuary.

The man with the vision and determination to carry out this monumental task was a salt tax inspector in Béziers called Pierre Paul Riquet. The idea of such a canal had been around since Roman times but the problems of creating a waterway through hilly terrain and without an adequate water supply in the dry season had prevented it being realised. Riquet believed he knew how to do it and he persuaded King Louis XIV to back it. His plan involved the creation of a large artificial lake, the St Ferriol Reservoir Map B1, in the Montagne Noire to provide a constant water supply for the highest reaches of the canal 50 miles away. The water from the mountains feeds the canal at Narouze where the watershed between the Atlantic and the Mediterranean lies. Here an obelisk in memory of Riquet was erected in 1825 by his family. When royal, financial support ran out, he used his and his wife's personal fortunes to continue the work, beggaring himself in the process. It took a labour force of 12,000 men 15 years to complete the immense task. Riquet died, ill and exhausted, just months before it was finished. It runs for 240 km (150 miles), has 64 locks, and 54 aqueducts, some to re-route rivers across it, the longest of which is the 190 metre long *Aquaduct de l'Orb*. One of Riquet's most impressive engineering feats (remember this man was a tax collector by profession, not a civil engineer) is the Malpas Tunnel. Instead of skirting round the Ensérune Hill, he chose to tunnel 173 metres through it. It was an amazing feat for the time. The canal served successfully as a mercantile route for more than 200 years but eventually with the coming of the railway it ceased to be used for transporting goods. One of the bargemen's overnight stops was at Le Somail which is still used for this purpose by holiday-makers. The village even has a grocer's shop on a barge, moored by the towpath. For bibliophiles it also has a *librairie ancienne*, an antiquarian bookshop, with 50,000 books in stock.

Initially the route of the canal bypassed Carcassonne to the north but this was rectified at the end of the 18th century. By then the canal had already become a route to be followed for pleasure too, and this is what it is now. Hundreds of large and small houseboats and cabin cruisers ply its waters giving pleasure to tens of thousands of tourists every summer. The tow-paths for the barges' horses have now become the preserve of early morning joggers, and walkers and cyclists.

The canal provides a slow, relaxing way of exploring the region, and not least of sampling wines from the scores of vineyards that are passed *en route*. The speed limit on the canal is just 5mph. There is no requirement for a sailing licence on the canal, but before taking control of a hire boat, you will be shown how to manoeuvre it and how to work the locks if there is no lock keeper. There are plenty of places to tie up for the night, such as Carcassonne, and the bigger places offer a variety of facilities for boats.

Boats can be hired for just a day or longer at a number of centres along the canal, including Homps Map D1, Le Somail Map E1/2, Trèbes Map C2, Carcass-onne Map C2 and Castelnaudary Map B1. Or you can take a *promenade en bâteau* for a couple of hours from either Homps or Carcassonne; a running commentary is given by a guide in French, English and Spanish about the history of the canal and its fauna and flora, and as you pass through locks you see at first-hand how they are operated. To give an idea of prices - a two hour cruise from Homps costs 12.40€ for an adult and 6.80€ for children aged between 3 and 12. Alternatively you could hire a cruiser for 4 people for 200€ for a full day. You can also hire electrically powered boats by the hour or half day at La Redorte Map D2 and at Port de Bram Map B2 See www.castelnautique.com

The *Aire de Port Lauragais* Map A1, a motorway rest area, on the A61 between Toulouse and Carcassonne is on the same site as a marina on the canal close to the watershed at Narouze. It has a cultural centre dedicated to Riquet which has an informative exhibition about the canal.

A newly opened attraction is the *Musée et Jardins du Canal du Midi* in the original home of Pierre-Paul Riquet close to the B*assin de St Ferréol* Map B1 in the Montagne Noire. The museum is set in a park laid out in the 19th century. It is a beautiful forested area with some lovely walks.

Philippe Calais who is a primary school teacher has produced an excellent website with a large collection of photographs of the Canal – they are the fruit of an educational project he did with a class of children many years ago. He has also published an informative guide for cyclists *Le Canal du Midi à Vélo*. See

www.canalmidi.com You will also enjoy www.midicanal.co.uk

One of the Aude Tourist Board's broch-ures is about *tourisme fluvial*, more particular-ly about the *Canal du Midi et de la Robine*. It lists all the places where you can hire boats and cycles, as well as the short boat trips along sections of the canal.

Wine Trails

The whole *département* of Aude is covered in vineyards. Despite the big drop in consumption of wine by the French (and a consequent drop in the number of road fatalities thanks also to a policy of stricter controls on drink-driving), winemaking remains the major industry in the region with several hundred vineyards producing eight *appellations controlées*. The Languedoc was once known for the vast quantities of cheap, low quality wine it produced. It is still the largest producer in France but the quality over the past decade and more has risen significantly and the best of its wines now compare favourably with the best from other regions and they are still cheaper. The *AOC (l'appellation d'origine controlée)* quality wines are: **Cabardès, Corbières, Fitou, Limoux, Malepère, Minervois** and **Muscat de Rlvesaltes**. **La Clape**, the peninsula near Narbonne and the neighbouring area of **Quatourze** are now marketed as **Coteaux Languedoc.** In addition winegrowers in the area close to the city of Carcassonne produce very good *Vins de Pays.* You will also find *Vins de Pays de l'Aude* and *Vins de Pays d'Oc*.

Wines vary considerably depending on a whole range of factors of which climate (sunshine, wind, and humidity) is an important one - **Cabardès**, for example, has two vintages: Atlantic (using Merlot and Cabernet grapes) and Mediterranean (using Syrah and Grenache grapes). This is true also of the **Malepère** wines. The soil's mineral content is another determining factor as is the age of the vines, the mix of grapes and the individual skills of the wine-makers. This all makes for some interesting wine tasting if you tour part of the region and stop at some of the vineyards, meet with those who make the wine, taste a tiny glass or two and buy a couple of bottles at each place when you find ones that you particularly like. The important words to look out for as you drive along are: *Cave* or *Caveau, Degustation* and *Vente* meaning wine cellar, wine tasting and wine for sale.

You might also like to visit one of the bigger specialist retailers or the show-place for a particular *AOC*, such as the one for **Minervois** wines at Le Chai-Port Minervois at Homps Map D1, where you can get advice on 170 wines of the Minervois region. Detailed Wine Trail brochures for the various *AOC*s are readily available in the tourist offices.

The **Minervois** region extends from the Montagne Noire in the north to the *Canal du Midi* in the south and the *Cité* in the west and is about 5,500 hectares in size. It is a real mosaic of landscapes with eight distinct sectors identified where a wide variety of grapes are grown. The village of La Lavinière Map D1 has its own *appellation communale* **Minervois La Lavinière (AOC Village)** as does the village of St Jean-de-Minervois Map E1 just over the departmental border which produces a wonderful sweet dessert wine: *Le Muscat de St-Jean-de-Minervois (Vin Doux Naturel)*.

Corbières   This region is best known for its full-bodied reds to savour with meat dishes. There are currently more than a hundred winegrowers in an area of over 6,500 hectares stretching from Carcassonne across the Corbières hills to the south. There is also a local high-quality *AOC* called **Corbières-Boutenac**. Find out more at www.corbieresweb.com One place to taste some of them is at Terra Vinea on a hill overlooking Portel-des-Corbières Map E3. It is in a disused gypsum mine 80 metres underground where about 1,500 barrels of local wine are maturing, produced by three co-operatives operating under the name of *Caves Rocbère*. There are guided tours (in French) followed by wine tasting. Also in the mine is an exhibition of tools used in wine making, a cooper's workshop and a mock Roman villa! See www.terra-vinea.fr

The **Fitou** vineyards which produce intense, fragrant red wines stretch from the steep hillsides of the southern Corbières to the coast where the village of Fitou lies Map E3. The village has its annual wine festival at the end of July. The nine villages of the *appellation* also produce an excellent AOC sweet wine called **Muscat de Rivesaltes.** See www.fitouaoc.com

Limoux Map C2 was famous for its sparkling white wines long before Champagne and it still provides a very acceptable and much cheaper alternative to it. Benedictine monks at the Abbey of St Hilaire produced the world's first *brut* in 1531, *Blanquette de Limoux* - a blend primarily of Mauzac, with some Chenin and Chardonnay, aged for at least 8 months after a complex production process. *Crémant de Limoux* is a variation of the same with more Chenin and Chardonnay. *Blanquette Mèthode Ancestrale* is a low alcohol (7%) variation using 100% Mauzac grapes. The *Sieur d'Arques* winery in Limoux which produces six million bottles of sparkling wine a year offers a short teaching session on wine tasting. Find out more at www.limoux-aoc.com

The **La Clape** plateau south of Narbonne produces fine wines. One of the vineyards there, the *Château l'Hospitalet*, was awarded the prestigious title of Best European Winery of the Year in 2012.

If you would like to have a couple of hours tutoring in wine tasting by an English Master of Wine, Matthew Stubbs offers this at the impressive Domaine Gayda Map B2 at Brugairolles near Limoux. He also shows how the wines of this region in France can challenge the best of the rest. His tutored tasting lasts two hours or you can take part in a two-day course. See his wine school website: www.vinecole.com

Check with the tourist office in Carcassonne if there are to be any *balades vigneronnes* whilst you are down there. This is a programme of visits to particular vineyards in the area where you will be taken on a two hour guided walk of the land followed by wine tasting and a meal. Advance booking is essential.

If you are here in the autumn you could attend one of the village wine festivals or the one in Carcassonne itself when *Place Carnot* is covered in tents promoting and selling the wines of particular local vineyards.

Recreational Areas & Outdoor Activities

If you are staying inland, you do not need to drive all the way to the coast to go swimming or surf-boarding. There are lakes with good recreational facilities much nearer. The closest is **Le Lac de la Cavayère** MapC2, pictured above, just 3 km from the *Cité,* known to some as *Carcassonne Plage* as it has sandy beaches. It is a beautifully landscaped reservoir created in 1988 following a fire in the area. There is a broad path around the lake's perimeter and the walk takes between one and two hours depending on your level of fitness. Along the way there are several small picnic areas with benches and tables in the shade of trees. Swimming is permitted but only in designated areas where there are lifeguards. You can hire pedaloes and canoes, play mini golf, or you can relax while the children enjoy themselves at the **o2Aventure parcours acrobatique forestier,** a high level forestry acrobatic course which is open to the public from 13 to 18. Their website has a short video showing what exciting things you can do. Fees vary from 8€ to 16€. See www.o2aventure.com Orienteering, mountain biking and horse riding are all allowed, and you can hire horses from the **Centre équestre**. It is easy to find the lake - take the D6113 out of Carcassonne heading in the direction of Narbonne and before Trèbes turn right on to the road signposted to the lake. A bus also goes there from Carcassonne.

Lapradelle Map C1 in the Montagne Noire provides similar facilities for walking and swimming and picnics. It has extensive parking close to the lake, toilets and a small café. Also in the Montagne Noire is the **Bassin de St Ferriol**, the main feed reservoir for the *Canal du Midi*. It is a beautiful spot with plenty of water activities: wind surfing, canoeing, sailing and pedaloes and the village has a number of cafés and restaurants. You can also go pony trekking through the forests of the Montagne Noire.

Lake Jouarre Map D1 lies between Homps and Olonzac and is one of the biggest expanses of inland water. A holiday village has been developed nearby. Swimming is permitted and lifeguards are on duty in the summer. There is a sailing school, and dinghies can be hired. The path alongside the *Canal du Midi* which runs close to the lake is great for cycling. Bikes can be hired from Homps.

Heading south from Carcassonne in the direction of the Pyrenees offers other opportunities for outdoor activities. In Limoux you can join a canoeing expedition along the River Aude - see www.canoe limoux.com Further south at Quillan, Alet and Axat there is canyoning and white water rafting through the gorges on the River Aude.See www.laforgedequillan.fr for more information. This is a residential centre which provides all the equipment necessary for the various outdoor activities. The one condition usually required of participants is that they can swim 25 metres and be submerged. **Sud Rafting** based at Point d'Aliès Axat is another water activity centre with a lot on offer. And one more, based at Puichéric and at Axat, is **L'eau-rizon** – see www.eau-rizon.org

Horse and pony riding can be done at **Domaine de Pommayrac** in the village of Verzeille between Carcassonne and Limoux. All levels are catered for - beginners are taught by a qualified instructor and those at intermediate or advanced level are also supervised – see www.pommayrac.com Hostel and gites accommodation is available. There is pony riding for children aged 3 to 12. **La Gontarende** at Cuxac-Cabardès Map C1 also offers pony trekking as well as tuition in horse riding. And you will find a **Mini-Ranch** on the outskirts of the village Villeneuve-Minervois Map C1. There are several other places in Aude where you can enjoy horse riding – local tourist offices will provide details.

Between Limoux and Quillan there is **ACCRO'Parc** at Alet-les-Bains Map C3. This is a forest trail high up in the trees pictured below - **Parcours Acrobatique Forestier**. Everyone has to do the beginners green trail under the direction of instructors in order to learn how to proceed through the trees safely; you then progress to the yellow trail which has 12 different games at a maximum height of 7 metres and finally to the red trail with 10 games between 4 and 10 metres above the ground. Admission: adults 20€ children under 12 17€

If walking is among your favourite forms of exercise you will be spoilt for choice. Many of the villages have produced attractive, free leaflets describing walks in their immediate vicinity. The European walking route **GR 36** which runs from Switzerland to Spain passes through Aude from the oak forests of the Montagne Noire in the north along part of the *Canal du Midi* and on through the Corbières to the south. The route passes the castles at Villerouge Terménès, Termes and Peyrepertuse. The Aude Tourist Department has published a free 24 page booklet about walking in the region and giving details of the maps you will need. It is called *Le Sentier Cathare Promenades et Randonnées*. See www.lesentiercathare.com

At the southern end of the *département* in **Aude en Pyrénées** there are 190 km of walking trails and 890 km of marked trails for mountain bikers, the largest

such area in the Pyrenees.

A new guide for walkers in the Upper valley of the Aude is *le Pays de la haute Vallée de l'Aude* which suggests 29 routes over the whole region. Cyclists see www.cyclo-pyrenees.com and www.vtt-pyrenees.com For more about the area including all its many sporting facilities, see www.aude-pyrenees.fr

Theme Parks & Animal Farms

Carcassonne's major attraction of this kind is just five minutes drive away from the *Cité* in the direction of Lake Cavayère. It is **Le Parc Australien** where you can get a taste of life in Australia with its display of wildlife from that continent. There are supervised activities for children such as panning for gold, learning to throw a boomerang or play a didgeridoo and much more. In the summer it is open from 10.30 - 19. Entrance costs 10€ for adults and 7€ for children. Out of season the park is usually open just from 14 - 18. Find out more at www.leparcaustralien.fr

Drive north from Carcassonne towards the Montagne Noire and you have a number of choices. Near Saissac Map B1 at **Picarel le Haut**, Catherine Sonef has been farming deer since 1986 and now has some 150 animals. Entry and parking is free at this working farm from 14. There are guided tours at 15 and 17 costing just 2 euros for adults, children under 10 are free. Many of the animals are very tame and will let you stroke them if you approach them quietly. The farm has its own simple shop and an auberge where you can enjoy a meal of *civet de daguet*, the succulent meat of very young stags bred there, accompanied by fresh vegetables, fruit and cheeses from neighbouring farms. See www.picarel-cerf.com

Near Castans Map D1 on the Route de Pradelles (D9) in a beautiful forested area you can visit **Les Lamas de la Montagne Noire**. These gentle animals from Chile are now being bred here and you can go on a short trek along one of the woodland paths with one of them. If you book in advance you can ask to have an English speaking guide. Open all year from 9 a.m. to sunset. The farm visit costs 5.50€ for adults, children aged 6 – 14 2€, a one hour trek in groups of at least four costs 10€ per person. See www.lamabalade.fr

By far the largest nature reserve is **La Réserve Africaine de Sigean** Map E2 which celebrates its 40th anniversary in 2014 about 15 km south of Narbonne off highway D6009. Expect to spend at least half a day at it. There are over 3,800 animals on site from the continent of Africa . Everything you would expect to see: elephants, giraffes, leopards, lions, rhinos, springboks, zebras and much more.

The visit falls into two parts: a six km drive through what are designated as savannah and bush areas where you can expect to see

big game – the biggest are a quartet of white rhinos - and then a two to three hour stroll which will take you past an island for chimpanzees, a small lake with flocks of flamingos, ibis, pelicans and many more species, and along the African plain dotted with lots of other wildlife, including buffalo and elephants. This game reserve claims to have more Tibetan bears than are left in Tibet! You can expect to get some good, close up photos of the wild life – ostriches and zebras roam across the roads. There is a strict instruction to keep the car windows closed and never to get out of the car. Resist the temptation to lower a window and take a picture when you are driving close to the pride of lions!

The park has kiosks and a restaurant, as well as indoor and outdoor areas for picnics. This is the most expensive of the animal parks and farms in the area: 31€ for adults and 22€ for children aged 4 – 11 but it makes a great day out. The park is open every day of the year from 9 to 18.30 in the summer and to 18 in winter. For more details see www.reserveafricainesigean.fr

The *Parc historique de loisirs en terre Cathare* is a very different kind of theme park located at the *Château de Chalabre* Map B3 between Mirepoix and Limoux. An Association known as *Les Chevaliers du Kercorb* has been renovating the castle and its adjoining park since 2002 and the knights now give children the chance to learn about and to experience a wide variety of activities associated with life in the Middle Ages, among them archery and heraldry,

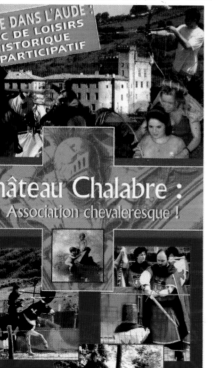

watching the knights in the jousting tournaments, taking part in dancing and games, as well as less vigorous activities such as calligraphy and iconography. It is open during the French school holidays at Easter and on Ascension Day, and during July and August from 12 - 18.30. Find out more at www.chateau-chalabre.com

Whilst not a theme park as such, lovers of falconry can see some impressive displays at Peyrepertuse castle Map D3 during July and August. Check their website for details of dates and times. It is an important element in the *Festival Médiéval* held there in early August. When it started in 2003 the festival attracted 3,000 visitors, by 2005 that had risen to 12,000 and numbers have continued to increase year by year. See www.chateau-peyrepertuse.com for details.

Sun, Sea and Sand

This stretch of the Mediterranean coast gets over 300 days of sunshine a year and with an average of just 12 mm of rain in July and 30mm in August. So you are more or less guaranteed dry, sunny weather. The truth, however, is that it can sometimes get too hot – temperatures of 35°c/ 100°f at midday are not unusual so it is advisable to stay out of the sun between 12 and 14 and to use high factor sunscreen when you are on the beach.

Most of the coastline is one long sandy beach or sandbar between the sea and inland lagoons, and the resort beaches have all won blue flag awards for their cleanliness. In the early 1960s the Government funded the construction of eight new holiday resorts along the Languedoc-Roussillon coast. Care was taken to protect the natural environment and not destroy it by over development. Their initiative has paid off as millions of French and foreign tourists now spend their summer vacations here but driving the A9 motorway at the start and end of the French national holidays in August can be hell. Be warned! Local papers publicise the days and times when the roads are likely to be most congested and suggest less trafficated routes.

Thousands of pine trees, tamarisk and laurels have been planted and much of the development is low-rise apartment blocks and holiday homes. Starting with Les Cabanes de Fleury on the edge of the La Clape massif, and running west in the direction of Spain, they are St Pierre-sur-Mer which merges into Narbonne Plage, Gruissan, Port-La-Nouvelle, La Franqui (the oldest seaside resort on the coast), Leucate Plage and Port Leucate which has one of the largest yachting marinas on the Languedoc coast.

The best of these resorts is arguably **Leucate Plage** Map F3. The beach of fine sand runs for 8 km with the sea on one side and the lagoon, the *Etang de Leucate ou Salses*, on the other. Frequent winds make this long lagoon ideal for windsurfing and kite surfing. In fact the wind blows here on 300 days a year. The annual world championship in windsurfing, *Mondial du Vent,* has been held here in Spring since 1996 – this year it runs from 26 April to 4 May. The event attracts about 250 competitors and over 150,000 spectators. See www.mondial-du-vent.com

North of Leucate is **La Franqui,** a small family resort at the foot of some cliffs (a rare sight on this bit of the coast) which provides shelter from the *tramontine* wind. Nearby is an immense, wild beach called Les Coussoules which is excellent for wind buggies. From the headland above La Franqui there are stunning views and this is a popular area for walking and mountain biking and hang gliding. See www.tourisme-leucate.fr

Port-La-Nouvelle Map F3 is very different. It was founded in 1820 as the commercial port for Narbonne to which it is linked by the *Canal de la Robine*. It is France's third largest port on the south coast. It also still has an active fishing fleet and fish market. Every morning from 9 you can buy freshly caught fish from the fishermen along the *Avenue de la Mer.* You can watch freighters, tankers, and fishing boats as well as admiring the pleasure boats of the wealthy for it is a pleasure resort too. Quite a mix for one small town. There is a wide beach of fine white sand (cleaned every day) which slopes gently into the sea. In the height of the summer season canal boats run from Narbonne to Port la Nouvelle past the islands of Nadière and Sainte Lucie. The latter is now a 250 hectare heavily wooded nature reserve with a marked botanical trail. For more details see www.portlanouvelle.com

Gruissan Map F2 is different again. In the Middle Ages it served as one of Narbonne's ports. It is a picturesque, traditional village built in concentric circles round a hill topped by the *Tour de Barberousse*, the remains of a 13th century castle which was built for protection from Turkish pirates. Then there is the modern holiday resort with its beach apartment blocks, yachting marina and restaurants, and thirdly there is *La Plage des Pilotis* which was featured in the cult film *Betty Blue*. This is the site of a collection of 1300 wooden chalets built on piles to protect them from the sea which regularly covers the beach here. An extra attraction this resort offers is deep sea fishing trips. Nearby, salt extraction is done on a large scale on the Ile de St Martin – follow the signs for **Salin du Midi** from Gruissan old village. During the holiday season you can take a guided tour round the salt pans and buy some of this natural product. There is a small museum-cum-educational centre about 'farming' salt from Roman times. The village also has an exhibition on bird migration and an observation point in a protected area. Since 2004 the village has had a centre for training profess-

ionals in the wine industry and part of it is also open to the public. See www.gruissan-mediterranee.com

Narbonne Plage Map F2 is another modern, family resort with a vast, wide sandy beach and offering plenty of activities, including in the summer tuition in Salsa and Latin dancing on Tuesday evenings. The beach runs for five km along the coast to **St Pierre sur Mer**, once a small fishing harbour but also now a marina and a growing holiday resort. Courses in kite-surfing and windsurfing are held here. See www.snkite.com The quieter end of this beautiful beach which shelves gently into the sea is just before the yachting marina on the edge of Narbonne Plage and St Pierre pictured on the left.

Museums with a Difference

Museums can be fun and provide an entertaining and educational alternative when a break from the beach or the hills is needed. Here are a few suggestions which are worth a visit.

In the village of Villeneuve Minervois Map C1 ten miles north of Carcassonne the Bénazeth family restored a disused windmill dating from 1819 to full working order in 2002. It is one of only two functioning windmills in the *département* of Aude and during the 45 minute guided tour you can see it in action making flour. There is an exhibition about the mill's 19th century history and about the reconstruction work. The Bénazeth family are wine-makers and you can taste their products at the reception centre. Their Plo de Roy vintage which is aged in oak barrels in the huge natural underground cavern, *le Gouffre de Cabrespine*, is particularly good. There is plenty of parking space by the mill and an attractive picnic area. Open 10 - 18.30 in July and August, 14 - 17.30 in May and June and 14 - 17 in April and September. Admission 5€ for adults, 3€ for children. See www.moulin-benazeth.fr Whilst in the village, take a trip down to the **Maison de la Truffe** situated behind the *mairie*. It is a small interactive museum about the local black gold: truffles.

Le Musée de l'Ecole at 3 *rue de Plô* in the *Cité* will bring back memories to older visitors as it covers school life up to the middle of the 20th century, and French schools weren't that different to British ones pre-World War II. In addition to recreating school life a century ago there is also a separate exhibition about France and her former colonies - some of which subsequently became British, notably Canada and India. Younger visitors will enjoy it too and may well appreciate their own very different school environment all the more when comparing it to how things were in their grandparents time. Open 10 - 18. The museum is accessible for visitors in wheelchairs.

Le Musée de la Chapellerie is at Le Somail Map E2 7 miles to the north of Narbonne. If you love hats, this is the place to visit as it houses a vast collection of headwear from 84 countries – there are over 6500 exhibits. Open 9 - 12 and 14 - 19 each day from June to September. For more details see www.musee-chapeaux. com

Le Musée Contemporain de la Chapellerie is another but quite different hat museum in the small town of Espéraza Map C3 south of

Limoux. A century ago it was the second largest manufacturer of hats in the world! Its 'golden age' was between the two World Wars when it had 14 factories employing over 4,000 people. Visitors are shown by means of video the whole process of hat making from the shearing of sheep right through to the finished and fashioned articles. Open 10 - 12 and 14 - 18.   Right next door is **Dinosauria Le Musée des Dinosaures** and the entry charge covers both museums. In 2003 the remains of a hitherto unknown kind of dinosaur was discovered in the neighbouring village of Campagne sur Aude and the museum shows an informative film about the excavation and subsequent reconstruction. There are a number of dinosaur remains on show as the region is rich in them. At Campagne Map C3 there is a paleontological dig site with a fossil workshop for children. See www.dinosauria.org

The 'book village' of Montolieu is home to hundreds of thousands of second hand books. It has a museum dedicated to the history of books and book pro-duction and holds temporary exhibitions of graphic art. See www.montolieu-livre.fr

Near Narbonne at 32 *quai de Lorraine* in the little wine village of Sallèles d'Aude Map E2 is **Amphoralis Musée des potiers gallo-romains**. This is an unusual museum in that it is built over a still unfinished archaeological dig.   A clear explanatory leaflet in English plus photographs and models in the exhibition hall makes understanding the site straight forward. Archaeologists have uncovered pottery kilns and a settlement from Roman times. Over the past decade they have been reconstructing ovens for baking pottery modelled exactly on those unearthed. The work goes on and visitors can join in it on pre-published dates. Amphoras from here, used in the export of wine from Nar-bonne, have been found as far away as northern Britain. The museum is open 1st July – 30th Sept 10 - 12 and 15 - 19. Opening hours are more restricted the rest of the year. Admission: adults 6€ and children 4€. www.amphoralis.com

Another specialist museum for those interested in history and music is **le Musée du Quercorb** at Puivert Map B3 to the south of Limoux. In addition to the several rooms illustrating daily life in Quercorb in bygone times there is an Intrumentarium where you can see reconstructions of 8 musical instruments from the 14th century the details of which have been taken from stone carvings in the Castle's keep at Puivert! A video presentation tells how this was done and you can hear them being played. The museum is air conditioned and there is an attractive picnic area. Open from mid-July to 31st August 10 -19, and from 11 April to Sept 10 - 12.30 and 14 - 18. See www.quercorb. com/mus

Lagrasse has a fascinating museum depicting life locally in 1900. Among its varied exhibits are 400 dolls! Open from 1 April to 15 October and during the Christmas holidays. It is situated on the main street. See www.1900-lagrasse.com

Enjoying Nature

In order to enjoy the sight, scents and sounds of nature you don't need to be a well read amateur botanist or a keen ornithologist but it will certainly add greatly to your enjoyment if you gain some knowledge as you explore and discover just how bountiful nature is in this part of the Languedoc. A good French handbook is *La Nature Méditerrenéenne en France* by Les Ecologistes de l'Enzième. It can provide you with the right answers when one of the family asks what the large bird of prey soaring on a thermal high above your head is or what herbs and plants are producing the wonderful scents of the *garrigue* which they can smell.

In the spring the roadsides are covered in wild flowers. In the summer heat the ground becomes very dry and arid with rather less to see, but by then the vines are rich in foliage and the grapes are appearing and many fields are full of sunflowers or poppies. There are, however, some nasties, so be prepared. The mosquito for one! And lots of other flying insects in the woods and *garrigue* which will enjoy biting any bare flesh you are showing which hasn't been protected by an anti-insect gel or spray. There are just two creatures which in theory could give you a serious bite: scorpions and adders, but the chance of encountering either of them is fairly remote.

Starting with the coast, parts of it are designated as nature conservation areas and you will see signs to this effect. See www.parc-naturel-narbonnaise. fr for details of walks in this area. The *Massif de la Clape* Map F2 between Narbonne and the coast is an area of rugged limestone, about 17 km long by 8 km wide, much of it covered by *garrigue* where you can find a fine range of flowers, including several kinds of orchids and wild roses. Over half of it is a protected area. It is a good place for seeing birds - among them some uncommon ones such as Bonelli's eagles, short toed eagles and eagle owls. And it is an area rich in butterflies. When you are ready for some refreshment, remember that La Clape has its own *appellation* and is particularly noted for its fresh white wines – you can visit the *Château de l'Hospitalet* on the D168 to taste some of them.

To the north of La Clape lies the **Etang de Pissevaches** (and yes, the name does mean cow piss!), a coastal lagoon with salt marshes which is a good area for bird watching especially at times of migration. The same is true of the lagoons around Gruissan. Between Gruissan and Port la Nouvelle you can visit the nature reserve of **Ile de Ste Lucie** Map F3. It has broad trails through its woods, ideal for walking or cycling. A narrow road from the edge of Port la Nouvelle which runs along part of the *Canal de la Robine* leads to the lock at the island where there is access to the marked trails.

Further south there is the limestone headland of Cap Leucate Map F3 which is rich in flora in spring as well as being a good spot for watching migrant birds, best seen between March – May, and mid-August – October. Bob Gibbons in his *Travellers' Nature Guide to France* describes what an exciting place this is for bird watching. He lists 'raptors such as honey buzzard, black kite, marsh harrier, short-toed eagle and a few ospreys'. Among the hundreds of thousands of passing birds, he mentions 'finches, bee-eaters, red-rumped swallows, pipits including red-throated warblers, and shrikes' and among the birds breeding locally the 'blue rock thrush, speckled and orphean warblers, short-toed lark, black-eared wheatear, hoopoe and occasional great spotted cuckoos.' Nearby are two lagoons, the ***Etang de Leucate*** and the ***Etang de Lapalme*** Map E/F3 where flamingos, avocets and many other birds can be seen. It is reckoned that you can see some 200 species of birds and 700 species of plants along this stretch of the coast.

A drive in the summer sunshine through the Corbières hills especially where the road goes through the *garrigue* is a memorable experience not least because of the wonderful smells from the shrubs and wild herbs. In late summer you will find wild fig trees hanging rich with fruit and can see lizards flitting across the rocks and hear the rustling of cicadas.

If you love walking among trees Aude offers you plenty of choice from the extensive beech and chestnut forests at Loubatiere and Ramondens near ***Le lac de Laprade*** Map C1 in the Montagne Noire to ***La route du sapin***, the road through magnificent pine forests near Belcaire Map B4 southwest of Limoux. At Saissac Map B1 there is a lovely park originally landscaped in the 19th century and the ***Arboretum du Lampy*** which has giant American Redwoods and Cedars of Lebanon among its many varieties of trees.

One of the loveliest places to visit is the botanical garden, ***La Bouichère Le Jardin aux Plantes***, on the edge of Limoux Map C2 near the LeClerc and Bricomarche stores. It is a very extensive garden with some 2,500 varieties of plants, many of them rare. It exhibits in fact many different types of garden, e.g. a medieval one, a kitchen and medicinal herb garden, an English border garden, a tropical area, a fruit garden, a spice garden, a bamboo area, a recently created rose garden, a pond area and much more – all laid out in such a way that you can really enjoy them. Benches are set in several shady areas, so you can sit and simply revel in all the colours, scents and beauty that surround you.

Admission is 7.50€ for adults, 4€ for older children but no charge for children under one metre high! Open June - August from 10 - 18 and May, Sept - Oct from 13 - 18 but it is closed on Mondays and Tuesdays.
See www.labouichere. com

Some Wonders of Nature

France has some of the most beautiful underground sights in the world. You can find two of them just north of Carcassonne in the Montagne Noire. The **Grotte de Limousis** Map C1 is a wonder-land of aragonite crystal formations, limestone curtains, scallop patterns on the ceiling, columns, stalagmites and stalactites and with some beautiful reflections in still pools. There is a 45 minute guided tour of the cave which stretches some 600 metres into the mountainside. The guides speak only French but a brief description in English printed on two sides of A4 paper is available from reception. Photography is permitted and there is a lot to photograph.

The tour ends in what is called the 'hall of chandeliers'. The most spectacular of which hangs 4 metres down from the ceiling and has a circumference of 10 metres. It is truly majestic. And by an imaginative use of lighting which focuses in turn on the several formations of aragonite in that hall to the accompaniment of some appropriate music, it serves as a fitting finale to what is a magical experience underground. The cave is open in July and August from 10.30 to 18, but has much reduced opening hours in the spring and autumn. It is closed from December to the end of February. Entry fee: 10€ for adults, 6.20€ for children. See www.grotte-de-limousis.com

Ten minutes drive away up the D112 through the *Gorges de la Clamoux* north of Villeneuve-Minervois is the ***Gouffre de Cabrespine*** Map C1, the deepest cavern in Europe and one of the deepest in the world. St Paul's Cathedral would fit in it very comfortably with space to spare. In fact you could fit two cathedrals in, one on top of the other! The route for visitors has been laid out in such a way that there are no steps, the paths simply slope down or up so it really is accessible for all. The view from the *balcon du Diable* is awe-inspiring - here is truly one of nature's wonders, the work of water on stone through millions of years leaving behind a myriad of beautiful stone and crystal formations. The standard tour lasts 45 minutes but for those with a special interest in caving and fit enough to take part, it is possible to book a place on a five hour long exploration and much lower down led by a speliologist. The Cavern is open in July and August from 10 - 18.30; reduced opening in spring and autumn, and closed in December and January. Entry fee: 10€ for adults, 6.20€ for children. See www.grottes-de-france.com

Sticking with the effect of water on the landscape, there are some spectacular gorges to drive or walk

through. The Michelin maps highlight the most scenic bits of any route by marking that stretch of the road green and there are plenty of them in the *département*. The River Aude above Quillan has created a number of gorges where the mountains rise dramatically on both sides, sometimes for several hundred metres, for example at the **Défilé de la Pierre-Lys** Map C4. Near **Axat** is the **Gorges de St Georges** Map C4 where it narrows to about 20 - 25 metres with 300 metre high cliffs. Higher still up the River Aude, the D118 passes the **Grotte de l'Aguzou** Map B4. The cave is open to the public but can only be visited by appointment.

The **Massif de la Clape** south of Narbonne is a beautiful wild area of limestone outcrops and *garrigue* but also with a lot of vineyards on the lower slopes. One of its most striking natural features is **Le Gouffre de l'Œil Doux** Map F2 pictured below – the 'Sweet Eye Abyss' – a deep pool of fresh water yet so close to the sea. On the D1118 about three miles north of St Pierre sur Mer there is a large, tree-shaded picnic area and car park which is the starting point for a 15 minute walk up a broad, rocky path to the edge of the cliff overlooking the pool. It can also be reached from below but swimming is no longer permitted in the pool.

There are thermal springs in the region which the Romans took advantage of to create spas. You can still enjoy the benefits of these naturally warm waters rich in minerals at Rennes-les-Bains in the Upper Valley of the Aude Map C3 Rennes is a picturesque little village and it has quite a large outdoor swimming pool (including a small children's pool). It can get quite crowded in summer and the changing facilities are a little basic but it is a lovely place to spend an hour or two. If you want to have a dip free of charge, you can walk down alongside the river to find one of the thermal water hotspots (usually a bit crowded). The spa is open from 3 March – 14 November in 2014. For more details of treatments, prices etc, see www.renneslesbains.com (French only). There are also a couple of decent places to eat in the village after you have enjoyed a swim.

There is another open-air thermal pool in Alet-les-Bains a few kilometres north on the main road which runs alongside the River Aude.

For the really high peaks and views from them you have to head to the southernmost part of the *département*, to the Pyrenees – to *Pic d'Ourthizat* at 1937 metres and *Pic de Madres* Map C4 at 2469 metres. But before you reach them there are some exceptionally beautiful landscapes of high mountain pastures and thick forests which in spring display a wonderful array of shades of vibrant fresh green. The area around the *Pic de Bugarach* Map C3 is one such spot.

Music Festivals

All the events illustrated here from previous pro-
grammes are annual events. For the latest information
about what is on culturally in the coming months in
Carcassonne itself, look at the city's website where you
will find a diary of events - www.carcassonne.org
When you are down here the local daily paper *Midi
Libre* has a column *Les Animations du Jour* which gives
details of all concerts, plays, conferences, fairs, book
signings, dances, lectures, children's activities etc that are on that day. You can
be almost certain of finding something which would appeal to you. Another
source of information for the wider region is www.audepyrenees.com

Carcassonne hosts a major arts and music festival in July each year with
concerts at various locations in the *Cité* and *La Bastide*. Last year a hundred of
the concerts were free. Only artists of national and international renown are
invited to perform. The 2014 programme is now available online – one of the
star attractions will be Elton John who will perform on 15 July. There are also
ballet, opera and theatre performances. See www.festivaldecarcassonne.fr for
full details. There are other shorter festivals throughout the year, e.g. a **Spanish
Week** is held at the end of August when concerts and dance performances are
given and there is opportunity to sample some Spanish gastronomic delights.

The magnificent organ in St Vincent's Church is played at several concerts
during the summer in an organ festival called **Les Vents d'Anges.** The former
cathedral in the *Cité* has its own annual series of organ concerts, **Les Estivales
d'Orgue de la Cité**. See www.estivales.org

In the winter and spring each year the *Chapelle des Jésuites* on *rue des
Études* in the lower city is the venue for a series of classical orchestral concerts
known as **Les Jeudis de l'Auditorium**. A few years ago the Chapel was fitted out
to provide optimal acoustics. And at the beginning of April it hosts a Jazz Week
– the 4 evening concerts cost just 40€ for all four.

You will also find concerts being held in abbeys, churches and castles out in
the sticks. The abbey at **Caunes Minervois** Map D1 is one such venue. It has a
regular programme of concerts held on Friday evenings at 21.30 followed by a
wine tasting courtesy of one of the local *vignerons*. The
series runs from early July to late August and includes
classical concerts as well as popular contemporary
music. Before each concert you can enjoy *une assiette
gourmande* and drinks in the gardens of the abbey but
advance booking at the local tourist office is necessary
for the meal. You can buy a ticket for a single concert or
a season ticket for all five concerts - children under 16
are admitted free. See www.caunes-minervois.com

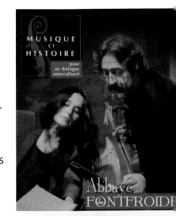

The *Abbaye Ste-Marie d'Orbieu* in Lagrasse Map D2 is
used for concerts during the area's **Baroque en Miner-**

vois series of concerts in June and for the ***Fuguepassiclassique*** music festival in July. The other concerts in this series are held in abbeys and churches throughout Aude – at Caunes-Minervois, in the Abbey de Villelongue, St Hilaire, St Polycarpe, Alet-les-Bains and the church in Ouveillan. The website to check is www.fuguepassiclassique.fr

The Abbey at Fontfroide Map E2 is another venue for great performers. Their 2014 programme includes their 9th ***Festival Musique et Histoire*** from 15-20 July with concerts by Jordi Savall and Montserrat Figueras. See www.fontfroide.com for more details.

The ***Festival de Fontcalvy*** Map E1 is a mix of theatre, music and comedy held between mid-July and mid-August in a former Cistercian fortified barn near Ouveillan. The shows begin at 22 but are preceded by a public, open air meal at 19.30. See www.festival-fontcalvy.com

Fourteen communes in the *Haute Vallée de l'Aude,* the upper reaches of the River Aude, sponsor an **International Festival of Folklore** at the end of July and beginning of August each year. For details of these and other cultural events in this part of Aude, see www.audepyrenees.fr Qillan, for example, is the venue for a Guitar festival in July and a Jazz festival in August.

Jazz festivals are to be found throughout the region. One that has become an established annual event in the Montagne Noire is ***Jazz sous les châtaigniers*** – Jazz under the chestnut trees. It is held in early August at the *château de Roquefère* near the famous cavern at Limoussis. For more details, see www.jazz-roquefere.com If you do go there, Roquefère has a good restaurant, the *Sire de Cabaret*. Lots of villages have a ***Fête de la Musique*** on 21 June when amateurs and professionals bring music to the streets.

Narbonne Map E2 has an arts festival called ***Festa Latina*** which runs from late June to the end of August and which celebrates the culture of the south through music, theatre, films, exhibitions, food and wine. Some of the events are held in Narbonne Plage. For details see – www.mairie-narbonne.fr Between September and April a monthly concert ***Musiques en Monuments*** is held on Saturdays at 16.30 in the Archbishops' Palace. See www.narbonne.fr And there is a free monthly organ concert between June and September. See www.les-orgues-de-narbonne.com

Some vineyard owners also play host to jazz and classical musicians – among them Gérard Bertrand at the *Château l'Hospitalet* on the La Clape headland Map F2 The restaurant is the venue for dinner-concerts at which regional jazz players perform. See www.gerard-bertrand.com Béatrice and Graham Nutter at the *Château Saint-Jacques d'Albas* which is a couple of kilometres from Laure Minervois Map D1 also have concerts occasionally with dinners. See www.chateaustjacques.com

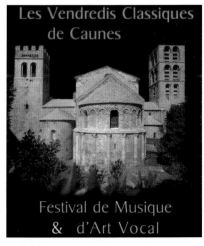

Les Vendredis Classiques de Caunes

Festival de Musique & d'Art Vocal

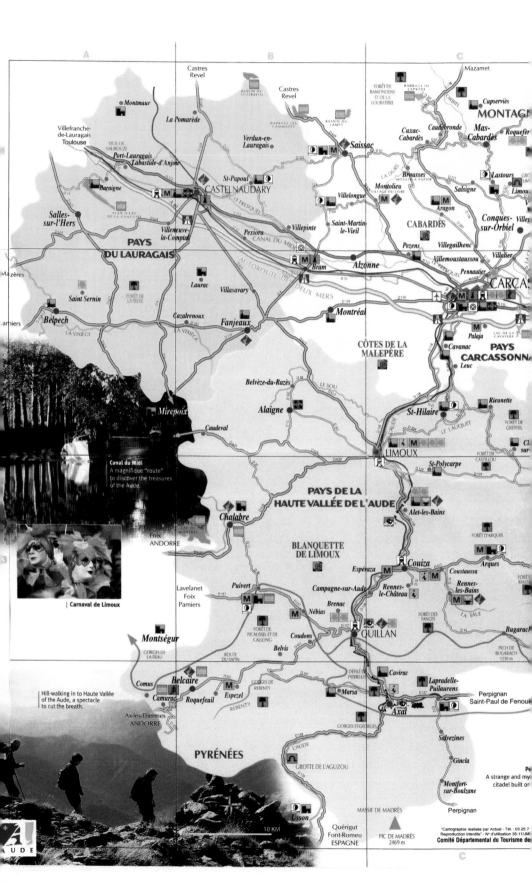

The Lands of Aude

LEGEND

Abbey/church	Tourist Board
Castle	Tourist Information point
Museum	AOC Wines
Cathar country major site	UNESCO World Patrimony
Historical monument	House of the Region Natural Park "la Narbonnaise en Méditerranée"
Natural site	Railway Station
Cave	Tourist train
Peak	Toll
Golf	Railway Network
Ski resort	Main centre
Pond	Site of special touristic interest
Lake	Motorway
Seaside resort	Main Road
White water sports	Secondary road (1 et 2ⁿᵈ category)
Spa	Secondary road (3ᵉ category)
Port and mooring point	Cathar trail
Nationwide flower decorated towns and villages	

Carcassonne Cité
The magic of the Middles-Ages, an UNESCO declared world heritage site.

The Mediterranean
Beaches of fine sand and authentic villages.

PAYS DE LA NARBONNAISE

PAYS CORBIÈRES-MINERVOIS

Shopping

Les Délices de Terroir is a sign you will often see in villages and occasionally at some of the sites you visit. It indicates that good quality local products are on sale there, usually foodstuffs of many kinds as well as wines, liqueurs, and confectionery such as nougat and pralines. There is a good choice of bottled or canned regional produce which will provide savoury memories of your holiday: stuffed olives, anchovies, foie gras, cassoulet, honey, olive products, and nuts.

All the really big stores such as *Géant*, *LeClerc*, and *Intermarché* are to be found in the commercial areas on the edge of town. If you are touring by car, it is in your interests to find them as petrol and diesel are significantly cheaper there than anywhere else. In fact just about everything is cheaper there, food, wine, clothes, electrical goods etc, and you can get a decent three course lunch for about 10€.

Unlike Britain, French shops do not have so-called 'Sales' (*Soldes* in French) on most of the time. There are just two fixed sales seasons a year, each one lasting five weeks. In 2014 the starting dates are the second Wednesday in January and the last Wednesday in June. Shops are also allowed to choose two further weeks but these short *soldes flottantes* must end at least a month before the start of the fixed ones. You can pick up some real bargains then, both in specialist shops and in the supermarkets. You will, however, often see goods marked down in price at other times or special offers even if it isn't an official sales week. Opening hours for shops are usually 10 - 19 and super-markets 9 - 20. They are not normally open on Sundays. Shops in villages and some in town close 12-14 every day for the traditional two hour break for lunch.

Honey comes in many flavours and a variety of forms, so why not visit one of the places that specializes in this natural product? One km outside the village of Montseret at Hameaux des Clauses Map E2 on the D423 there is a beekeepers co-operative which welcomes visitors. It is called **Miellerie des Clauses**. One of the beekeepers will be happy to talk about their work and answer questions, and one of the staff speaks English. On show is a transparent hive so you can see the bees at work inside. You can taste honey in a variety of flavours — acacia, flowers of the garrigue, rosemary, and many more, or sample a small glass of mead along with a piece of honey cake, or buy some honey soap! It is only a small place but worth a visit. Look out for the yellow signs along the road to it. It is open every day from 9 - 12 and from 14 - 18, and you can take part in an hour long free guided tour. See www.miellerie-des-clauses.com

One speciality shop that many shoppers will want to patronise is the **Chocolatier**. France has some of the world's finest chocolate makers. It is a highly skilled profession and their products are truly scrumptious. There is a *chocolatier* in Carcassonne on the *Place Carnot* and in the *Cité* you will also find

a large sweet shop, **La Cure Gourmande**, which children will like. If you are touring in the upper valley of the Aude, there is an excellent *chocolatier* at Luc sur Aude near Couiza Map C3 called **Nougalet** and another award winning one in Quillan, **Confiserie LUMEL**. Another sweet product made locally in the villages of the Montagne Noire are *Carbardises* delicious caramelised walnuts, hazelnuts and almonds – definitely 'more-ish' for nut lovers.

Still on the subject of food, the French love their bread - a meal is lacking if there is no bread on the table. Many villages still have their own **boulangerie**, bakery, selling fresh bread in many shapes and sizes, *ficelles, baguettes longues* or *court, flutes, pain de campagne* or flavoured in some particular way such as *pain au noix*. Newly baked bread is available early morning, noon and evening. There are also several kinds of *brioche* and *viennoiserie*, sweet soft bread, as well as a range of delicious cakes and pastries.

Another shop for those who enjoy their food is the **traiteur** or delicatessen where you can buy ready-made meals prepared on the premises. In addition to the specialist shops of this kind in town centres, you will find such departments in bigger supermarkets.

There are few departmental stores in town centres, **Monoprix** is the exception in Carcassonne but there is no shortage of specialist shops: clothes boutiques, lingerie, hats, leather goods, shoes, jewellery, perfumes, soft furnishings, toys, mobile phones, etc. Bookshops are called **Librairies**, and English newspapers (a day late) are usually available wherever you see the word **Presse** above the shop.

Mention has already been made of the fruit and vegetable markets on *Place de Carnot* in Carcassonne. You will also find a good range of other specialist food products there such as Catalan sausages, cheeses and all kinds of marinated olives. There is also a very large cheap clothes market along the *Boulevard Barbès* on Tuesday, Thursday and Saturday mornings.

The Romans introduced the olive tree to the region and olive oil is still an important constituent of local cooking. The only olive cooperative in Aude is the **Coopérative l'Oulibo** at *Bize Minervois* E1 founded in 1942. The olives grown here are called *Lucque de Bize* and are regarded by connoisseurs as being among the best. You can taste them, prepared in different ways, at their shop. It also has a good range of other local products: honey, goat's cheese, cooked meats, nougat, wines and brandies, as well as items made from olive tree wood.

In addition to the shop, they have an educational attraction called **L'Odyssée de l'Olivier** which starts with a guided tour through olive groves and then moves on to a working mill which produces olive oil. The fee for the guided tour is adults 6€ and children 3€. In July and August it is open from 8 to 20, the rest of the year from 8 - 12 and 14 - 19. www.odyssea.eu/oulibo/

Arts and Crafts

If you have time for just one craft shop, then make it **la Coopérative Artisanale du "Vieux Lavoir"** on *rue du Plo* in Carcassonne's *Cité.* Here you will find an excellent selection of beautiful goods hand made by craftsmen in the region: pottery, leather, glass, metal, linen, silk, paintings and much else. It is a real treasure trove of a place. It has information leaflets about several of those who have made the goods. Details are given of where their workshops are to be found should you want to pay them a visit to see more of their work or even perhaps to commission a particular piece as a special gift.

Another place in Carcassonne which has a 'concept store' selling designer clothes and pottery is at the restaurant *Jardin en ville*. A friend, who loves eating there, said about it, "You can go in for a coffee or lunch and come out with an embroidered velvet coat or some designer pots."

Some of the tourist sites that attract lots of visitors such as particular castles or abbeys have art and crafts exhibitions during the summer months. The **Château d'Arques** Map C3, for example, pictured below has exhibitions of particular painters a fortnight at a time from the end of May through to the end of August.

The **Abbaye de Villelongue** Map B1 is host to an exhibition of **sculptures dans les jardins** from April to October and during the summer it has an art exhibition in the refectory. The village of Montolieu has art and photographic and sculpture exhibitions at **La Coopérative,** its **Centre d'Art et de Littérature**

Many of the small towns and villages you may pass through as you tour the region will have signs indicating that *artisans*, craftsmen, are based there. Potters are the most common and you can often watch them at work. The word to look out for is *poterie*. Dominique Devouard is one of them whose workshop and showroom is open throughout the year from 10-12 apart from Sunday mornings and from 15-20. You can find her at **Poterie des Pontils** on the *Route d'Arques* at Peyrolles Map C3. The well-stocked shop there also sells pottery by other craftsmen. There are so many beautiful pieces, you are unlikely to leave

without having first bought something.

Another pottery is that of Lionel Postal at the northern end of Caunes Minervois Map D1. The town also has a painter's and sculptor's studio (Jean Michel Lafite) and a marble workshop. Caunes,

naturally, has its own Festival of Sculpture and Marble which in 2014 will be held in June. You can watch a short video of the 2013 festival on their website See www.lesmarbrieresdecaunes.fr .

The village of Minerve Map E1 is another spot for potters and artists where you can buy some beautiful mementos of your visit.

The art festival *Chemin des Artistes* has been discontinued and been succeeded by *Artistes a Suivre*. Their festival which is held in a number of locations in the Upper Aude Valley runs from 29 May – 1 June. For details see www.artistesasuivre.org

On the D168, the road from Narbonne to Narbonne Plage, which runs through the La Clape peninsula Map F2 you pass the **Château de l'Hospitalet** which is now a three star hotel owned by Gérard Bertrand, a former Narbonne rugby star. It also houses a variety of art and craft workshops as well as a wine centre, a museum of historical curios and an art gallery. There is a programme of international art exhibitions which changes every second month, and in the summer there is a festival of classical music and a jazz festival held in the castle courtyard. And, as you might expect, a *restaurant gastronomique* and a *bistrot*. See www.gerard-bertrand.com

The small town of Lagrasse Map D2 as well as being listed as one of the most beautiful villages in France is also labelled a **Ville et Métiers d'Art** because of the large number of artisans with workshops there: craftsmen in wood, leather, metal, ceramics, stained glass, jewellery, and designers of clothes and furniture.

The neighbouring village of Mayronnes has an unusual annual Sculpture Trail **Sentier Sculpturel** which opens on 7 April and lasts until 26 September. See www.sentiersculpturel. com

You will often find artists, potters and sculptors displaying their work at the autumn wine festivals in the towns and villages all over the region. Sometimes you can see several of them at work in the same

place. At the Caunes Festival of Sculpture and Marble, for example, you can watch sculptors in ice as well as marble, clay and wood, and workers of wrought iron. Quite a mix and not to be missed.

Eating out

Food is taken seriously in France and is a frequent topic of conversation! Shop-keepers are usually ready to advise on how to prepare and cook what you have bought from them. I remember the first time I bought asparagus from a stall-holder in Carcassonne market. Seeing that I was not French, he immediately volunteered information on how best to prepare the vegetables he had grown. And when my wife first bought some slices of home cured ham in our village shop which the shopkeeper had just cut for her, he insisted that she took a melon to go with it which he chose for her as he wanted us to enjoy our lunch in the way he himself would at home.

A word of caution: the quality of restaurants is variable. Many foreign tourists come to France expecting to eat very well at any local restaurant but that is an unrealistic expectation. Eating out is not particularly cheap in France any longer either. Read menus carefully, take a discreet look at what is being served and even the expressions on people's faces! Cafés, brasseries and restaurants always display their menus outside the building so that you can see what is on offer and what it will cost you. There will often be three or four *Menu Fixe* or *Formules* at various levels and prices. It is always cheaper to eat at lunch time when a simple menu of *entrée, plat du jour*, and *dessert* or coffee is on offer. Few places have menus in English though some do, so it is worth asking. Here are some of the dishes you might see listed:

Entrées*:*

Soupe de l'oignon - onion soup, *soupe de poissons* - fish soup, *potage aux légumes* vegetable soup. *pâté de foie gras* - liver pâté, *pâté maison* - home made pâté, usually of pork. When melons are in season, they figure as an *entrée*, served either with cured ham or filled with sweet Muscat wine or port.

Two other common options are: *Cruditées* - a plate of chopped raw vegetables – and *charcuterie*: a plate of sliced cooked meats. Bread is always served but without butter. It is customary in France to wait till your meal arrives before tucking into the bread!

Salades*:*

Sometimes the salad simply has a name, e.g. *salade composée, salade Nicoise* or *salade Cathare* and you may have to ask the waiter what is in it but often the menu will list all the main ingredients, lettuce, beans, onions, tomatoes, eggs, and anchovies, or whatever. A French salad is usually a substantial plateful - almost a meal in itself.

Pizzas:

The ingredients are usually listed, e.g. *trois fromages* might have the three cheeses: *chevre, cantal* and *roquefort*.

Viandes or ***Grillades****:* you will be asked how you want your meat cooked:

bleu very rare – *saignant(e)* rare – *à point/ rose* medium or *bien cuit* well-done.

Most meat dishes come with potatoes, usually *frites* but also *sautées* or *dauphine*..

Top of the local meat specialities is the white bean stew *cassoulet* using the Castelnaudary recipe which has pieces of shoulder of pork, sausage and preserved duck or simply with duck though many restaurants have their own variation of this favourite and substantial dish. A similar one is *Fricassée de Limoux* made from white beans and with ham. Sirloin steaks figure on many menus and come with a variety of sauces, *entrecôte au poivre* and *entrecôte au Roquefort* being two of them. *Magret de canard,* breast of duck is another regular dish. Omelettes of many kinds are available – a rather special Audoise dish is *omelette d'asperges sauvages* – made with local wild asparagus.

Children's menus:

Steak hachée is a minced beef burger and figures regularly on children's menus as do chicken nuggets. A 'fast food' dish which also often appears is *saucisse de Toulouse avec frites* - it is a bit like Cumberland sausage with chips

Desserts:

iles flottantes – squares of marshmallow in custard; *crème caramel* or *crème catalan; mousse au chocolat;* various *tartes* e.g. *tarte aux pommes,* apple pie. *Mouilleux* is a rich, soft chocolate cake. There is usually a separate ice cream menu (not cheap) or cheese may be offered as an alternative to a dessert in a fixed price menu. More expensive *menus fixes* will include a cheese course which usually consists of two or three small pieces of local cheeses.

Coffee is extra and unless otherwise requested will come in a tiny cup. If you are wanting milky coffee, ask for *un grand café crème.* You may also be asked if you would like a *digestif* such as cognac or a local brandy. The house wine, served in a ¼, ½ or 1 litre jug called a *pichet*, is usually a drinkable cheap local red, rosé or white wine. The bill is *l'addition.* The service charge and taxes are almost always included (TTC). Take time over your meal! The lunch break lasts two hours 12-14. Expect to spend longer in the evening when the meal will be more expensive. Dinner isn't usually served much before 19.30.

In addition to the many bars and brasseries serving simple, tasty food, there are some fine restaurants which serve regional dishes. One such is *L'écurie* at 43 *Boulevard Barbès* which is in a renovated 18th century stable in Carcassonne – see www.restaurant-lecurie.fr Another well recommended one is *Le jardin en ville* at 5 *rue des Framboisiers* - www.lejardinenville.fr One of my favourites is the *Domaine Gayda* down the Aude valley in the village of Brugairolles. It is a gourmet restaurant, pictured below, which serves excellent food at a leisurely

pace in a lovely setting overlooking rows of vines stretching to the distant hills See www.domaine gayda.com

There are also a few Michelin starred restaurants, among them *La Barbacane* with a single one in *La Cité* and *Le Parc* at 8 *Chemin des Anglais* which has two stars.

Towns & Villages of Interest

The large town of **Castelnaudary** Map B1 is best known for being the home of the regional dish *cassoulet* which is one of France's most popular meals. The local food factories produce 150,000 tins a day to meet that demand. There are plenty of restaurants and other food outlets in the town where you can buy it. Half-day *cassoulet* cookery courses are held in the autumn. Whilst the older part of the town does not compare with the *Cité* in Carcassonne it does have some lovely old buildings, notably the *Presidial*, once a courthouse and prison, with its beautiful Renaissance frontage built on the orders of Catherine de Medici, Queen of France and Countess of the Lauragais. Castelnaudary was once an important commercial port on the *Canal du Midi* but its *Grand Bassin* is now home just to pleasure boats. See www.castelnaudary-tourisme.com

Mirepoix Map A2 is situated just outside Aude in the Ariège but is such a delightful place and so near, it has to be included. Head for the ancient part of the town, a typical *bastide*, where there is plenty of parking near the medieval cathedral which is worth a look inside. The town is most famous for the wooden arcades around the square pictured above which adjoins the cathedral and for the very many fine carvings on the beam ends jutting out above the arcades, mostly dating from the 12th and 13th centuries. You will find some good shops and cafés here. The town hosts many events which attract large numbers of visitors, among them an antiques fair and puppet festival and in late July a medieval tournament – ***les Médiévales de Mirepoix*** which includes a concert and a ball. See www.ot-mirepoix.fr

Limoux Map C2 is another attractive town situated to the south of Carcassonne. The tourist office is on the main road the D118 and there is free parking across the road from it. A short walk takes you down into the town centre where you will find a pretty square with arcades round it. It is here that the revellers parade and sing and dance at weekends during what must be the world's longest carnival - it lasts from January till a fortnight before Easter and has been an annual event since the Middle Ages. Driving into town you cannot mistake what is its biggest export: the original French sparkling wine *Blanquette de Limoux* and a stop for sampling some is a must for any visitor. Limoux is also known for its fine nougat. There are some medieval remains notably the parish church of St Martin and parts of the 14th century town walls. The tourist office on the *Promenade du Tivoli* is at the same location as the *Musée Petiet* which has a beautiful collection of French paintings from *la belle Époque*. On *Place du 22 Septembre* in the *Eglise St Jacques* is France's only museum devoted solely to pianos and their manufacture - it has about 60 of them but it is only open for a limited period in the summer. See www.limoux.fr

A much visited small village on top of a hill in the upper valley of the Aude is **Rennes le Château** Map C3 – see www.rennes-le-chateau.fr Despite the beautiful views to be had from the hilltop, it would probably never have figured on any tourist's itinerary had it not been for the book *The Blood and the Holy Grail*. I prefer the historic village of **Alet-les-Bains** nearby which is much more interesting with more to offer. As has **Rennes-les-Bains** with its thermal baths (five hot springs and four cold ones) and its open air thermal pool.

Lagrasse Map D2 is counted among the most beautiful villages in France. It has a lovely setting on the river Orbieu. In addition to its famous abbey (see page 10) founded by Charlemagne, it is rich in medieval buildings. The market place pictured above is especially fine. And it has some good craft shops and restaurants, and an unusual museum about life locally in 1900. It is definitely worth a visit. Another beautiful village is **Minerve** Map E1 where 140 Cathars were burned alive in 1210. It is sited on a rocky spur dominating the gorges of the rivers *La Cesse* and *Brian*. Parking is outside the village.

Narbonne Map E2 is the largest town in the *département* with a history as old as that of Carcassonne. The Romans made it the capital of their first colony outside Italy and it quickly became famous for its wine exports. You can still see a small part of the **via Domitia** in the square near the Cathedral, and the underground storage rooms of that era, the **horraeum**, can be visited. The *Musée Lapidaire* houses an extensive collection of Roman remains - one of the best in Europe. Work begins in 2014 on building a huge new regional museum to house the 15,000 items of sculpture, mosaics, murals and everyday articles from the ancient world which they have. The cathedral begun in 1272 was intended to be the largest in France and a symbol of the Catholic Church's power but only the chancel was completed. The former residence of the Archbishops, the *Palais des Archevêques*, next door to the cathedral is open to visitors and it has a fine archaeological museum with an impressive collection of frescos and mosaics. The town has its own canal, the *Canal de la Robine*, which links up with the *Canal du Midi*. There are lots of good shops, an extensive market on both banks of the canal, and many eating places. The town boasts an Olympic size outdoor swimming pool heated to 27°c at the *Espace de Liberté* see www.espaceliberte.com Other amenities on the same site include indoor pools, an ice rink, bowling and a skate park plus a restaurant. The town has a lot going for it but street parking in the centre can prove difficult. A centrally

located underground car park is *Les Halles – Mirabeau*. *Les Halles* is the very large and lovely indoor market pictured left. See www.mairie-narbonne.fr

Touring in the Region

Be sure to have a full tank of petrol or diesel if you are heading off into the countryside, there is an absence of petrol stations out in the sticks! It is easy to get caught out. Driving in low gear along winding, hilly roads uses a lot of fuel. Road surfaces are generally good even on minor D roads but they can be very narrow and many French drivers like to drive fast, so be warned! In case of an accident requiring medical assistance, contact the emergency services: *service d'aide médicale d'urgence* is 15, Police 17 and Fire *Pompiers* 18. In addition to the normal road signs used all over the EU, many French towns and villages have created their own for reminding drivers to slow down and drive carefully through their village – see the one pictured above which you will see as you enter Peyriac-Minervois. They carry a serious warning in a colourful and sometimes amusing way.

There is no shortage of hotel accommodation in the region but the chains of cheap ones such as *Etap*, *Formule* 1, and *Première Classe* are only be found on the outskirts of the larger towns. Narbonne and Carcassonne have the full range from cheap hostels to luxurious five star hotels. Elsewhere you will find modest one or two star hotels, and occasionally more expensive ones in converted *châteaux*. In the villages you are more likely to find small inns, a*uberges,* or *gîtes* belonging to villagers or *chambres d'hôtes* where eating with your hosts may be an option. The main website for *gîtes* is www.gites-de-france-aude.com More information about accommodation is on page 54. However limited your knowledge of spoken French may be, don't be afraid to try it out. Many owners do not speak English or very little, and they will be very pleased if you make the effort to speak their language.

Many farms now do B + B and/or have *gîtes* or have a permit and all the necessary washing and toilet facilities for camping on their land. Farms are normally limited to just 25 pitches for tents or caravans, so you can be fairly

sure it will be quiet and peaceful. A few of them also offer an evening meal and at many more you can buy fresh produce grown or made on the farm. The Aude Chamber of Agriculture has published an attractive and informative booklet entitled **Bienvenue à la ferme dans l'Aude**, 'Welcome to the Farm', which gives full details. Copies are available from tourist offices. They also have a website at www.bienvenue-a-la-ferme.com Driving along you will often see signs for *chambres d'hôtes* and occasionally at vineyards which will give you the added bonus if you stay there of discovering first hand something of the science of wine making. Many of the

chambres d'hôtes are checked and commended for quality by the regional board. You will see a sign outside indicating what their rating is. Ex-pats too are now doing this as it is one of the few means open to them of being self-employed and making a living. Many have their own websites. If you are toying with the idea of moving to the region, you might find it helpful to stay with an ex-pat family who can tell you how they have coped with the move and the change of culture and they can explain something of the formalities and requirements which are inevitably a part of relocating to a new country.

The Tourist Office has leaflets and booklets about routes tourists may wish to follow - wine routes in particular. Also popular is *la Route des Cathares* which takes you to all the castles and sites related to the Cathars and the Catholic Church's crusade against them in the 13th century. On pages 46 –50 you will find 6 routes I have devised which include many of the sites recommended in this guide.

As you enter a village there is often a sign indicating how many pedestrian crossings *'passages'* there are on the road and how many 'sleeping policemen' *'ralentisseurs'* you will bump over. If there is something of particular interest in or near the village such as pre-historic dolmens, a pre-Roman iron age hilltop fort or a medieval tower there will usually be a special sign indicating this. In most villages, you can expect to find information boards telling visitors what shops etc are to be found - see above. You may also find either a map showing the footpaths and marked trails in the immediate vicinity of the village or a colourful map or poster of the wider area such as the one pictured below.

An alternative mode of transport to the car is the *autorail touristique du Minervois* which runs in the summer season from Narbonne to Bize Minervois. There is also the *train touristique Trans-Vallées Express* which runs from Rivesaltes in the *département* of Roussillon to Quillan in Aude. This one allows you to get off at a couple of points and make excursions by bus to the *Gorges de Galamus* and the Castle of Puilaurans. See www.tpcf.fr

Seasons of the Year

Carcassonne and the coastal resorts can get very crowded in July and August. If you can come a bit earlier in spring or a bit later in the autumn you will enjoy it even more, and the temperature of the sea is still warm enough for swimming. Christmas too is a good time to visit as lots of extra events are laid on in the lower town. An ice skating rink is rigged up on the *Place Carnot* and there are log cabins selling seasonal fare at a **Marché de Noël**, and there is live music to be enjoyed at it.

Even in the winter months there are special events. Most towns and villages have Christmas markets. The villages of Moussoulens Map C1, Talairan Map D3 and Villeneuve Minervois Map C1 each have three **Foires au Truffes** between late December and early February. There is usually a chef at these events describing ways in which to use truffles in your cooking. And there is plenty of other good local produce on sale at them. Puicheric Map D2 has a pig and wine festival **Fête du cochon et du Minervois** in January.

Many villages arrange communal New Year parties called **Reveillon de Saint Sylvestre**. The local mayors and councils host dinner parties in the New Year for all the senior citizens in their villages. Occasionally, though rarely, there can be a heavy snowfall down on the plain – there's no shortage of it, of course, in the Pyrenees.

Spring is celebrated with a number of festivals especially in wine villages and at particular *domaines* and *châteaux*. As you drive through villages you will see posters advertising - **Printemps du Minervois** or whatever the local wine is and giving the details of events. They provide a chance to meet some of the local *vignerons* and sample their products.

Another spring event is the village **Foire des Fleurs** or flower market where you can stock up on all the flowering plants and bushes you need for the garden or the balcony. Watch out for signs as you drive into villages about when theirs is. This is sometimes organised as a fund-raiser for the local village school or sports centre.

The harvesting of almost any crop is a good enough reason for a festival, so in May when the first local cherries are appearing, expect to see a **Fête de la Cerise** advertised. The village of Trausse-Minervois Map D1 has its in mid-May.

These fairs and festivals offer far more than a simple market, though you can of course expect to buy whatever product is being celebrated. They often include

C'est le printem du Minervois

lectures on the product, guided walks in the vicinity and the opportunity to share in a public, celebratory meal open to anyone, though advance booking is usually required.

You will be surprised what can be celebrated! Limoux Map C2, for example, has a triennial festival in August in honour of a particular breed of cow, **Fête de la Gasconne**, when the main road through town is lined with temporary cow byres for a weekend and you can enjoy freshly roasted beef sandwiches from street stalls. Bize-Minervois Map E1 has its **Fête de l'Olivier** in mid-July. One of the biggest festivals is the **Fête du Cassoulet** at Castelnaudary Map B1 over the last weekend in August. It isn't just about eating, there are free concerts every night, water games on the Canal du Midi, wandering musicians, activities for children and a food and wine market. See www.fete-du-cassoulet.com

Harvesting the grapes, **Vendange**, which is spread over several weeks is hugely important in village life and when all is safely gathered in, it is time to party. During the harvesting, expect to get stuck on the roads behind small and slow moving tractors (top speed is 25 km) pulling loads of grapes. Whilst most vineyards have gone over to mechanical picking, a few still do it by hand and all the family get involved. Carcassonne, Lézignan and Limoux all have their **Fête des vins primeurs** in October as do many of the villages in Aude.

Citou Map D1 celebrates its locally grown sweet onions on the first Sunday in September at its **Fête de l'Oignon doux de Citou.** Mirepoix has its apple festival over a weekend in mid-October. The village of Aigues Vive Map D2 celebrates three products at the same time at its **Fête de la Pomme, du Vin et du Riz.** Castans celebrates its Chestnut Festival over the last weekend in October. Many towns and villages hold a **Foire au Gras** (literally a Fat Fair but meaning such things as plump poultry) – among them Caunes Minervois and Limoux in November, and Castelnaudary, Belpech and Rieux-Minervois in December. At these you can stock up for Christmas as you will find the pick of locally produced food and drinks on sale at them.

Village fêtes mark the seasons. Although Church and State are separated in France and many French people are now secular in spirit, Church festivals are still important including that of the local village's saint in whose honour their parish church is dedicated. The Christian festival of All Saints on November 1st is a public holiday and a day when you will see almost all the family graves in the local cemeteries covered in flowers, usually chrysanthemums. Remembrance Day, November 11th, is a national holiday and there is a short ceremony at the war memorial in most towns and villages – but not always at 11 a.m., so check

the time if you plan to attend.

Autumn brings a rich variety of colours in the vineyards – different types of vines turn a different colour: yellow, gold, brown and shades of red, before the leaves fade and fall. Then the cold winter winds blow and nature seems to die. The landscape, however, is still so beautiful.

Relocating to the Region

You have had a wonderful holiday and seen what a very attractive part of France this is. Maybe you spent some time window shopping outside estate agents and picked up some property brochures and now are excitedly contemplating the possibility of moving down here for good. Take your time before making the decision! It is a huge one and fraught with factors you may not yet have considered sufficiently. It will be worth reading the first hand accounts of others who have made the move. A good place to start is by subscribing to magazines such as *Living France* or *France* which regularly publish such stories. They also feature excellent articles on the practical aspects of buying and renovating property as well as offering guidance about finance and the French tax and inheritance laws.

Then there are plenty of books written in the last ten years by expatriates which describe their experience. This way you will discover lots about living in the region which at present you don't know, much of it very positive and encouraging but also highlighting some of the very real difficulties which can be encountered, not least if you are hoping to work here. Jobs are very hard to come by as unemployment is very high. One of the worst obstacles is French bureaucracy. Form-filling and engaging in face-to-face encounters with French officials who do not speak English can be a real headache. If you are not fluent in French, start language classes at once!

If you are still keen, you may now want to move on to something more technical and detailed such as the current edition of David Hampshere's *Living & Working in France*, or *The Complete Guide to Living in France* from the publishers of the magazine *Living France*. If your situation allows you to do it, come and live down here for some weeks out of the normal tourist season – hiring a gîte will be much cheaper than in the summer, and it will give you the opportunity to experience what living in a village or town down here is like as well as giving you plenty of time to explore particular towns and villages where you feel you would be happy and could settle into the local community. It will also allow you to practise and improve your French. If you are concerned to establish a network of expatriate friends, there's time to do that too. If you take time over the whole process, you are much more likely to get it right and to make the best decision about where to live.

It might be of help if I tell you how the process of relocating worked out for us. We had visited different parts of France on holiday over the years but found ourselves being drawn back to the Languedoc-Roussillon region again and again, usually in the early autumn when the weather was still good but far fewer visitors were there. At one stage we considered buying a small studio apartment in a new development at the holiday resort of La Bacarès but a year or so later we experienced just how crowded it can get in the high season along the coast and that put us off the idea. Soon afterwards we decided to explore the possibility of buying an old property inland but sufficiently close to the Mediterranean so that we could easily make day trips there. We spent one holiday looking at particular towns and villages which appealed to us, some of them in the Pyrénées-Orientales. For us, one important issue was the availability of flights nearby on low-cost airlines. Two such airports existed at Perpignan and Carcassonne, and both were close to motorways and had mainline railway stations. We then did a lot of homework via the internet. We spent many an evening accessing the websites of estate agents and looking at properties in our price category. In the end we settled on a long 'short list' of about a dozen properties situated within a 30 mile radius of Carcassonne. Just after Easter one year, my wife and I flew down to take a closer look at them. Three of them happened to be on the books of the same estate agent in Carcassonne, so we decided to start with that one. We never got any further. We were extremely fortunate in that the member of staff we dealt with spoke excellent English. She was a model of patience and we spent two and a half days with her driving round and looking at more properties than the three on our list from that agency. In the end we settled on an old house in a wine village which had once been the home and workplace of a *vigneron*, and a tiny vineyard outside the village came with the house. The village was clearly a 'living' one with a primary school, several shops, good sports facilities and much to commend it, not least that the residents clearly took pride in the appearance of their village. Among the shops was what one should expect to find in any good French village – a bakery! And there is a post office, a resident doctor and a dentist.

The house was in need of major restoration which took two years to complete. We used local craftsmen and as we would not be living locally during the period of the renovation, we decided to employ a manager for the project who could keep us informed by email of the progress of the work. We chose a *notaire* based in Carcassonne to do the legal work, one that the vendor who lived in Paris was happy to accept. We opened an account with a local bank as soon as we had signed the *compromis de vente* in order to make money transfers easier and to be able to pay all the builders bills with French cheques in euros. The legal work took about three months and we had to transfer the full price plus legal fees to the *notaire* before we all met in her office to initial and sign page after page of the contract. We also had to provide evidence to the *notaire* that we had insured the house from the date of the transfer of ownership. Since we bought our house new regulations have come into force which require the seller to provide the purchaser with reports on lead, asbestos, flood zones and in some areas termites. An energy efficiency report and a natural disaster risk report are also mandatory. Whilst the work was in progress we were spared having to pay the *taxe d'habitation* but we had to pay the annual *taxe foncière* which is based on the number of rooms and other facilities in the house. When the work was completed, the house was re-valued for taxation purposes which meant a significant increase.

We have had no regrets about the decision we made to buy a house in the region. Our neighbours have been very welcoming and friendly. Developing a network of French and expatriate friends, however, does require effort but it is not too difficult. Villages and towns have large numbers of *associations*, i.e. special interest activity groups, which are glad to welcome new members.

Six routes that take in some sites recommended in the Guide

The Michelin regional map is recommended. Road numbers for each route are given but once you leave the D6113, the main road out of Carcassonne, their numbers change so often you may find it easier to simply look for the name of the next village on your route on the signposts. There are lots of places to visit on each route, so you may well prefer to miss out some and spend longer at just a few of them.

Tour 1: Lagrasse, the Corbières hills, the castles at Queribus, Peyrepertuse and Puilaurens, the Gorges de Galamus and the Défilé de la Pierre-Lys.

You will need to start early if you are going to visit all the sites suggested. It is a long drive (about 130 miles) but with lots of interesting places to see, starting with one of the most beautiful villages in France followed by some spectacular castles and wonderful scenery.

Leave Carcassonne on the D6113 signposted to Narbonne. Just before Trèbes, turn right on to the D3 signposted to **Lagrasse** (see pages 10 + 39). From Lagrasse take the D212 south, turn left on to the D23 and then right on to the D613 signposted to **Villerouge-Terménès** (see page 9). Carry on to Félines-Terménès, past the village turn left on to the D39, then D139 signposted to Davejean, D410 to Maisons, D123 to Padern, D14 to Cucugnan, and the D123 to the **Château de Queribus** (see page 8). Go back down the hill and back down the D123, turn left on to the D14 to Duilhac-sous-Peyrepertuse. Park below the castle and climb up to the **Château de Peyrepertuse** (see page 9).

Back to the D14 and carry on to Cubières-sur-Cinoble, turn left on to the D10 for the **Gorges de Galamus** and the Ermitage St-Antoine de Galamus, then the D7 to St-Paul-de-Fenouillet, where you turn right on to the D117. At Lapradelle turn left on to the D22 for the **Château de Puilaurens**, park and climb up to the castle (see page 8). Back to the D117 and turn left for Axat, join the D118 signposted to Quillan, drive through the narrow **Défilé de la Pierre-Lys**. After Quillan follow the signs for Limoux via Espéraza, Couiza and Alet-

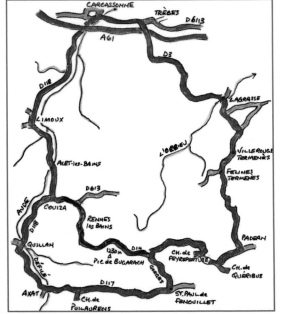

les-Bains. Stay on the D118 through the large town of Limoux and follow the signs for Carcassonne.

An alternative and shorter route (marked in blue on the map) for the last part of the journey would be to carry on along the D14 after Cubières-sur-Cinoble to Bugarach and Rennes-les-Bains (stop for a swim in the open air thermal pool), turning left at the junction with the D613 which brings you to Couiza and the D118 for Limoux and Carcassonne. This route takes you through some beautiful upland scenery around Bugarach though at times the road is very winding and you cannot afford to let the scenery affect your concentration on the road!

Tour 2: The mill at Villeneuve-Minervois, the giant cavern at Cabrespine, the abbey and marble quarry at Caunes-Minervois, the village of Minerve, the Canal du Midi and Chai at Homps, and Lake Jouarres.

This tour is about 90 miles. Take the road out of Carcassonne signposted for Mazamet, at a major roundabout take the D620 signposted Villalier, Villegly and Caunes Minervois. Turn off left on to the D112 for **Villeneuve-Minervois** and follow the signs for the **Moulin** (see page 22). On leaving, drive back through the village centre to rejoin the D112 for Cabrespine. You follow the gorge of the River Clamoux for about 10 kilometres then turn left up the hill to the giant cavern **Gouffre de Cabrespine** (see page 26) – where the last guided tour of the day is at 17. Then back down to Villeneuve-Minervois and follow the sign for **Caunes Minervois**, the D111, back to the D620, turn left for Caunes (see pages 10 + 35). Follow the sign for *centre ville* and the car park in front of the mairie. It is a short walk to the Abbey and then up the hill to the potter's studio. Return to the car park and go back to the main road through the town, the D620, and on the outskirts of town turn left along a track for the car park near the marble quarries, which are just a short walk away. Return to the town centre to find the D115 signposted for Trausse and on to the junction with the D52, turn left and follow the signs for Siran, Cesseras, Azillanet and **Minerve**. Parking is outside the village close to the bridge giving access to it. From Minerve continue on the D115 to La Caunette and on to the junction with the D907 signposted to Aigues-Vives, turn right down a short minor road to Aigne and turn right on the

D910 signposted to Beaufort, Olonzac and **Homps**. The roads in the village centre of Homps can be confusing as well as narrow but follow the signs for the Canal

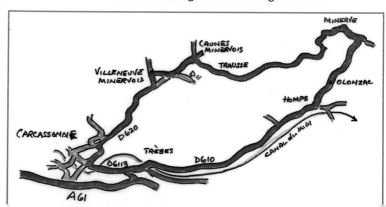

and you will soon arrive outside the old warehouse which is now the Chai, the centre for Minervois wines (see page 14). You can take a ride on a canal boat from here or hire a cycle to ride along the Canal. Or if you fancy a swim, **Jouarres Lake** (see page 16) is just a mile away with a sandy beach. Return to Carcassonne via the D610 to Puichéric and Trèbes where you meet the D6113.

Tour 3: St Hilaire Abbey, Limoux and the Aude valley, Puivert Castle and Lake Montbel

This route is about 90 miles. Follow the signs out of Carcassone for Limoux which will bring you on to the D118. After Rouffic-d'Aude turn left on to the D110 signposted Pomas and **St-Hilaire** (see page 10) where parking is a short walk away from the abbey. Take the D104 signposted for **Limoux** (see page 38). There is parking off the main road, the D118, across from the tourist office and the Petiet Art Museum, and it's just a short walk down in to the town centre. Afterwards, head south on the D118 along the valley of the River Aude where you can hire a kayak or go water rafting (see page 16) to Alet, then on to Couiza where you can make a detour on the D52 up the mountain to Rennes-le-Château made famous by the novel and film *The da Vinci Code*. Then comes **Espéraza** with its dinosaur museum and hat factory museum (see pages 22- 23). The dinosaur trail is nearby at Campagne-sur-Aude. At Quillan, turn right on to the D117 signposted to Nébias and **Puivert** for the castle with its 35 m high keep and Quercorb Museum (see page 23). There is a small lake with a beach close to the village centre, if you fancy a swim. Take the D120 signposted to Rivel and on to the junction with the D620, turn left for Ste-Colombe-sur-l'Hers, and turn left on to a minor road signposted for **Montbels** which will bring you to the lake. Take the D18 signposted to **Chalabre** (see page 19), which after the town becomes the D620 and leads to Limoux town centre where, if you didn't do it earlier, you should stop and taste some the town's famous sparkling wine (see page 15). The D118 takes you back to Carcassonne.

An alternative route after Couiza is to take the D613 (marked in blue on the map) and head out to **Arques** (see page 34) to see the castle there, and take a walk in the forests nearby. You could also combine this with the detour to Rennes-le-Château mentioned above. Return back along the D613 to Couiza, turn right on to the D118 and head back to Limoux and Carcassonne.

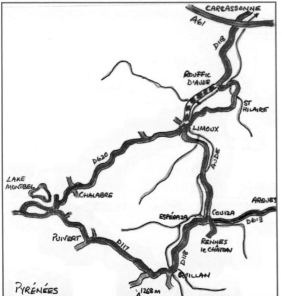

Tour 4: Narbonne, the Clape massif, Narbonne Plage and Amphoralis at Sallèles d'Aude.

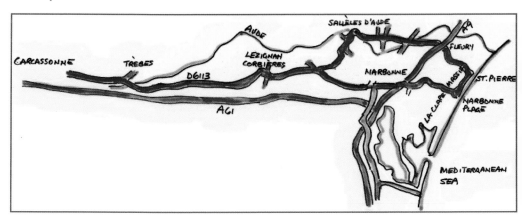

This route is about 105 miles. Take the D6113 from Carcassonne to **Narbonne**. Park in the town centre near the open air market (see page 39) for easy access to the cathedral and museums and the Canal de Robine. Getting out of Narbonne can be a headache but follow the signs for *autres directions* until you see a sign for **Narbonne Plage** which should lead you on to the D168 over the **La Clape massif** and past the **Château de l'Hospitalet** (see page 35) before you drop down to the coast. Turn left heading in the direction of St Pierre and turn off right to park by the beach (see page 21). In St Pierre take the D1118 inland and you will come to a tree-shaded parking area on the right hand side of the road not far from the **Gouffre de l'Œil-Doux** (see page 27). Continue on the D1118 to Fleury and Salles-d'Aude where you turn left on to the D31 for Coursan where you join and cross the D009 to pick up the D1118 for Cuxac-d'Aude and on to **Salleles-d'Aude** for Amphoralis, the Roman pottery museum. (see page 23). Back to the D1118 to St-Marcel-sur-Aude, then left on to the D607 to Marcorignan and a minor road which links to the D6113 signposted to Lézignan- Corbières, and on to Carcassonne.

Tour 5: African Safari Park and the beaches at Port-La-Nouvelle and Leucate Plage

An alternative to the above coastal trip is to head for the African Safari Park followed by some sun, sea and sand at Leucate Plage or

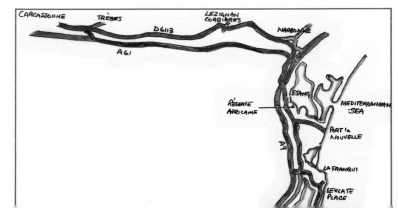

at Port-La-Nouvelle. This tour is about 140 miles but almost entirely along fast, major roads. Take the D6113 in the direction of Narbonne and on the outskirts join the D6009 signposted for Perpignan or take the motorways A61 and A9 down to junction 39. After the turning for Peyriac-sur-Mer on the D6009 comes the signpost for the **Réserve Africaine** (see page 18-19), turn left on to the approach road to it. If you haven't already visited Terra Vinea (page 15) at Portel-les-Corbières, you can do that after the Safari Park – the D611A leads to it. Take the road back to the D6009 and head south for the beaches – either to **Port-la-Nouvelle** (see pages 20-21) if you haven't already been there or go a bit further south to the resorts at **Leucate Plage** and **Port Leucate** (see page 20) via the D627.

Tour 6: Montolieu, Saissac Castle, St Papoul Abbey, Castelnaudary, Mirepoix and Montréal.

This tour is about 75 miles long. Leave Carcassonne heading west on the D6113, after Pezens fork right on to the D629 to the book town of **Montolieu** (see page 34) and on to the castle at **Saissac**. Not far away is the deer farm at Picarel le Haut (see page 18). From Saissac take the D103 signposted to **St Papoul** (see page 10). You can park in the square right outside the Abbey. Continue on the D103 into the centre of **Castelnaudary** (see page 38). If you haven't yet feasted on *cassoulet*, this is the place to do so. Take the D6 out of the town south to the beautiful, medieval town of **Mirepoix** (see page 38) where there are some good shops in the square by the cathedral, and there is parking nearby.

Return to Carcassonne via Fanjeaux where St Dominic founded his first religious community and Montréal. **Montréal** was where Cathar and Catholic theologians met in 1207 to argue the merits of their faiths – Dominic took part on the Catholic side. The town's Collegiate Church of St Vincent with its vast

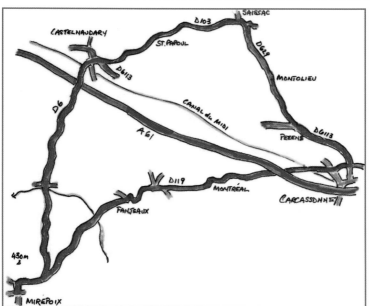

Gothic nave and beautiful 18th century organ is worth a visit. The church was founded by Pope Jean XXII in 1317.

Practical Information

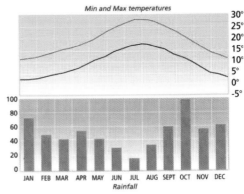

When to go

If the weather is a major consideration for you in determining when to visit, here is an overview of average temperatures and rainfall through the year. May and September are lovely months in which to come not least because there are fewer visitors and there is much less traffic on the main roads to and along the coast. The daily papers have a large local weather map on the back page every day – in summer it usually looks like the one reproduced below. Sun, sun, sun.

Getting there

By Air:

From the UK and Eire there are direct flights to Carcassonne with Ryanair from Bournemouth, Cork, Dublin, East Midlands, Glasgow Prestwick, Liverpool and London Stansted. See www.ryanair.com for booking.

The airport website is now also in English www.aeroport-carcassonne.com/en and gives an overview of schedules in addition to other useful information. The airport is compact and easy to find your way around. There is an information point, an ATM and a restaurant. There is a car park just across the road from the main entrance which is free for the first 15 minutes. Expect luggage checks (weight, dimensions) to be fairly rigorous on departure from this airport as well as from other small airports in the region.

Other Airports :

There are other airports within reasonable distance of Carcassonne: Béziers with Ryanair flights from Bristol, Edinburgh, London Luton and Manchester, see www.beziers.aeroport.fr Perpignan Airport is served by Aer Lingus, Flybe and Ryanair with flights from Dublin, Shannon, Birmingham, London Stansted and Southampton, see www.aeroport-perpignan.com/en. Toulouse is about 90km from Carcassonne and has a major international airport with several airlines flying to it from the UK. Girona Airport across the border in Spain is about a 3 hour drive from Carcassonne.

By Train:

Carcassonne station is located in the centre of the lower town. For all train information see the website for the French railway SNCF at www.sncf.fr Carcassonne is served by a number of

intercity and local trains. It is possible to travel to Toulouse, Bordeaux, Marseille, Lyon etc. There are direct day and night trains from Paris (Austerlitz) to Carcassonne taking about seven and a half hours. The motorail service from Calais to Toulouse no longer runs although there is a *Service Auto Train* which allows you to put your car on the train in Paris and pick it up again in Narbonne or Toulouse, see www.autotrain.voyages-sncf.com/dynamic/autotrain-webapp/homeControl.action A brochure in English can be downloaded from this site.

By Car:
It is a very long drive from any of the Channel ports to Carcassonne – the routes from Calais, Boulogne or Dunkirk using the motorways south all take about 10 hours driving (excluding stops for rest and refreshment). From St Malo it is shorter but the Channel crossing takes much longer and is more expensive. For help with routes, see www.theaa.com, www.rac.co.uk, and www.viamichelin.com. It is best to break the journey half way – there are plenty of cheap hotels situated close to motorway junctions. I prefer to use the Channel tunnel train from Folkestone to Calais; it is fast and with convenient access to motorways on both sides of the Channel. See www.eurotunnel.com for details of times and prices.

Getting around

To/from the Airport:
A shuttle bus, *Navette,* runs to/from the centre of Carcassonne stopping at the railway station and at the medieval *Cité*. A timetable is available on the airport website. The fare is currently still at 5€. There is a taxi rank directly outside the airport terminal building, tel: +33(0)4 68 71 50 50. Taxis are not that plentiful in Carcassonne so **don't** rely on being able to flag one down an hour before your plane leaves. Taxis can also be booked online at: www.taxi-carcassonne.fr/

Getting around Carcassonne:
Agglo provides the municipal bus service. Details of routes and prices can be seen on www.carcassonne-agglo.fr/-Transports-et-deplacements-.html (French only). Alternatively the tourist office will give you information on how to get to where you want to go. A single ticket valid for 1 hour costs 1€ (*ticket blanc*). A day ticket (*ticket bleu*) costs 2.60€, and a carnet of 10 single tickets costs 8€ (*ticket jaune*). A 'Navette petit train', small tourist train, runs between the lower town and the *Cité*. A single ticket for this is 2€ and a return ticket 3€. From May to September it is possible to get around the lower city by small electric vehicles called *toucs*. Timetables are available online at: www.carcassonne-agglo.fr/Navettes-et-TOUCS.html

Getting around the region:
For getting around the region by bus, a journey planner is available online at: http://audelignes.cg11.fr/index.php See also www.teissier.fr Cars Teissier serve a number of villages in the Minervois, the Montagne Noire and the Corbières. They also advertise a couple of regular *circuit touristique* trips to such destinations as the Minervois and Lastours castles. Ask at the tourist office for more information. For buses to towns in Aude (Narbonne, Limoux etc) see also www.keolisaude.com.

Information about regional train services is available at www.ter-sncf.fr or from the railway station in Carcassonne Map B1 – tel:04 68 71 79 14. There are a dozen trains a day to Narbonne and even more in the opposite direction to Toulouse, and five a day up the Aude Valley to Limoux, two of which go further to Quillan. Ticket prices for public transport within Aude have come down, and many operators are now offering flat fees of 1€ per ticket, including the local train service to Limoux and Quillan.

A *navette* from the airport to the upper valley of the Aude calls at Limoux, Alet-les-Bains, Couiza, Espéraza and Quillan - for booking see www.aerobus-hautevallee.com or phone 04 68 20 15 54. More information on regional travel is available from the tourist office or the bus companies. Between June and October the tourist office also runs a number of guided bus tours to some popular sites in the region. These are not cheap, however, 30-40 euros per adult, children under 15 half price, children under 6 free, more information on www.carcassonne.org or from the tourist office.

A number of private companies offer trips around the region to see sites which are difficult to reach without a car such as the Cathar castles. Ask at the tourist office for current recommendations. Such trips are often pricey, however, and do not always include entry fees or lunch.

Car Hire:
It is possible to get around the city and further afield using public transport. However, you might like to list which sites you want to visit and do some research to find out if these destinations can be conveniently reached by public transport. If you wish to do a lot of touring in the region hiring a car is a convenient option. Car hire firms have offices at Carcassonne Airport and in the city centre. If you are arriving on a Ryanair flight, it is worth looking at the cost of hiring a car through their partner Hertz, see www.ryanair.com Pre-booking a car is not a bad idea whichever firm you use as the queues at the car hire desks at the airport can sometimes be bothersome. Otherwise, you can always jump on the *navette* and hire a car in the city centre. Avis has an office conveniently located near the railway station. Remember that most shops and offices close for lunch between 12 - 14.

Canal Cruiser Hire:
Cruising along the *Canal du Midi* is a wonderfully relaxing way to see part of the region. Cruisers can be hired from a number of locations – see www.croisieres-du-midi.com or www.audetourisme.com for details. For short sightseeing trips, boats leave from the 'port' near the railway station in the lower town; sightseeing trips are also available from Homps and Le Somail.

Cycle Hire:
Cycling is a very popular sport in France, more so than probably anywhere else in Europe, so you will find cycling routes publicised by the local tourist offices in many parts of *Aude*, and you can hire cycles in many of the towns. Philippe Calas set up a web site in 1999 for people wanting to cycle the length of the *Canal du Midi* – see www.canalmidi.com - and two years later wrote a guide book for cyclists *Le Canal du Midi à Vélo*. www.velomellow.com is another useful website for people wanting to cycle along the Canal.

For cycling holidays in the upper valley of the River Aude, see www.vtt-pyrenees.com and www.cycleaude.com. If you just want to do a short organized trip, the tourist office advertises an organised cycle ride around Carcassonne in peak season. At Laure Minervois, a wine-making village in a very pretty setting about 20 minutes from Carcassonne, you can do an hour's cycling through vineyards, see www.domainefontanillehaut.com

Accommodation

Hotels which are part of the cheapest chains such as *Formule* 1, *Etap* and *Première Classe* are usually located on the outskirts of town – expect to pay about 35€ for a room, breakfast is extra. One chain which has hotels of various levels of comfort and cost is www.accorhotels.com. There is a good overview of accommodation possibilities with contact details at www.carcassonne.org It is possible to find a room in the *Cité* itself even if you are on a limited budget. If you are thinking of a weekend break in Carcassonne between November and March, you can take advantage of the *operation bon weekend en ville* hotel offer which gives you two nights for the price of one at selected hotels. Eight 2 and 3 star hotels in Carcassonne belong to the scheme. See www.tourism-carcassonne.co.uk/news/operation-bon-weekend-en-ville for information.

To book a *gîte*, see www.gites-de-france-aude.com where you can get details of properties in the *département* of Aude and also of people registered to provide Bed + Breakfast *Chambres d'Hôtes*. A room in B + B houses is likely to cost between 60€ and 80€ a night, though some are cheaper and a few are much more expensive. Some owners also offer an evening meal *Tables d'Hôtes* at an extra charge but not all do this. The agency has a brochure giving details of all those registered with them and their grading and price. The grades are marked with one to four arrowheads and you will find a plaque outside each registered property showing its grade.

There are also a number of advertising agencies which provide details of properties for hire, such as www.bvdirect.co.uk, www.cheznous.com, and www.ownersinfrance.com but they do not take responsibility for the quality of the properties and you have to rely on the owner's description being accurate.

Tourisme & Handicap

The Aude Tourist Board publishes a booklet **Tourisme & Handicap** listing hotels, restaurants and other sites which are wheel chair accessible and which make provision for those with other disabilities. Supermarkets usually have a checkout which gives handicapped customers priority in the queue. You will see this sign outside sites which are wheelchair accessible and equipped to help visitors with other disabilities.

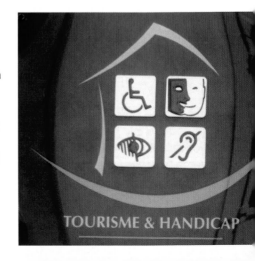

Public holidays/*Jours feriés*

January 1	*Jour de l'An*/New Year's Day
May 1	*Fête de Travail*/Labour Day
May 8	*Fête de la Victoire 1945*/Victory Day
July 14	*Fête Nationale*/Bastille Day
August 15	*Assomption*/Assumption of the Blessed Virgin Mary
November 1	*Fête de Toussaint*/All Saints
November 11	*Jour de l'Armistice*/ Remembrance Day
December 25	*Noël*/Christmas Day

and other major Christian festivals which have variable dates: *Pâques*/Easter (and Easter Monday), *Ascension* and *Pentecôte*/ Whitsunday. Shops do not open on these days.

Church Services

Local parish churches are Roman Catholic and services are, of course, in French. Both Carcassonne and Narbonne have cathedrals. Mass is usually celebrated at 11 on Sundays but also at other times and often on Saturday evenings.

The Anglican congregation which formerly met for worship in Limoux now uses the RC church in the village of Alet-les-Bains; the church is on the main street near the ruins of the Abbey. The Sunday Service starts at 10.30. Cars can be parked outside the church – see http://churchinmidipa.org There are also English language Protestant services at 10.30 in Homps and in a small chapel at the *Centre Paroissal* at the rear of the Cathedral in Mirepoix – see www.english churchmirepoix.org Two Anglican Readers, Adrian and Judy Wilson, now offer spiritual retreats at their home in Bezilhac. See www.spiritofangelsretreat.co.uk

Night Life

Most tourists don't come to the region for its night life but if you want to go clubbing and dance the night away there are plenty of venues where you can do this. The free entertainment provided in the summer in the beach resorts includes lots of open air concerts and dances. The newspaper *L'Independent* has an inset (*Le Journal de l'été*) every day during July and August listing everything that is going on in the region including all the live music events. Many restaurants and bars stay open till about midnight. After that it is over to the night spots, the *bars de nuit*, some of which stay open at weekends until 5 next morning.

Local Tourist Information Offices

Unfortunately, not all tourist offices have websites where you can access local information but all of them do stock a wide range of brochures. In the country they are still often called *syndicat d'Initiative*; in towns they are usually called *office de tourisme*. See the next Unit for website details.

If you are planning to visit several of the Cathar Country sites it is worth buying an **Intersite** card (2€) which gives you a 1 euro reduction at each of the 19 sites covered by the card. It is even better value for children as admission to

all the sites is free for children with a card. Reductions in admission charges at other tourist sites are usually only given to children and students.
See www.payscathare.org/en/sites-passport

Emergencies
Make sure you have the EU health cover card with you and show it if you have to visit a GP, hospital, clinic or dentist – you can normally obtain about 70% reimbursement on presentation of your receipted bills at the local CPAM office – the refund is sent to you later at your home address. If you are driving to the hospital look out for the road signs: usually a large letter H in red with a smaller red cross and an arrow indicating which way to turn. The Saturday local papers give details of which chemists are open over the weekend – in *Midi Libre* look for *EN CAS D'URGENCE* where you will find all the essential phone numbers for the emergency services, hospitals, chemists, etc.
Three numbers worth noting are:
Emergency medical aid *SAMU service d'aide médicale d'urgence* is 15,
Police 17 and Fire *Pompiers* 18.

Four good books to whet your appetite
Kate Mosse's trilogy of historical novels set in the area: *Labyrinth* 2006, *Sepulchre* 2008 and *Citadel* 2013. And a history of the Cathars: *The perfect Heresy* Stephen O'Shea 2000

Some language basics
Do not expect to find shopkeepers or the staff at the sites you visit fluent in English. They are much more likely to expect you to have some knowledge of French and when you do try to speak it, however badly, you will find that they will then all the more willingly try out their limited English. Why not brush up your French or do a basic course in the months before you travel At the very least I recommend that you buy a simple phrase book and learn how to greet people, how to ask for directions or order a meal in a restaurant, etc.
Failing all else, you have the absolute bare

 minimum on page 60. And as you explore the region, you will quickly begin to recognise and understand words and phrases that you see on signs and posters and shops. You can probably guess what these signs are saying to motorists.

Useful Websites
Most of these sites have an English language version

Tourism
www.audetourisme.com
www.aude-pyrenees.fr
www.carcassonne.org
www.corbieres-sauvages.com
www.payscathare.org
www.carcassonne.culture.fr

Accommodation
www.bienvenue-a-la-ferme.com
www.gites-de-france-aude.com

Transport
www.aerobus-hautevallee.com
www.aeroport-carcassonne.fr
www.aeroport-perpignan.com
www.beziers.aeroport.fr
www.carcassonne-agglo.fr
www.voyages-sncf.com
www.eurostar.com
www.eurotunnel.com
www.ter-sncf.com
www.tpcf.fr
www.viamichelin.com
www.croisieres-du-midi.com

Particular Tourist Sites
www.abbaye-de-villelongue.com
www.amphoralis.com
www.tourismecanaldumidi.fr
www.canalmidi.com
www.castelnautique.com
www.chateau-arques.fr
www.chateau-chalabre.com
www.chateau-peyrepertuse.com
www.chateau-de-puivert.com

www.cucugnan.fr (for Queribus)
www.dinosauria.org
www.grottes-de-france.com (for Limoussis & Cabrespine)
www.labouichere.com
www.lagrasse.com
www.1900-lagrasse.com   (for the museum)
www.lamabalade.fr
www.miellerie-des-clauses.com
www.moulinapapier.com
www.moulin-benazeth.fr
www.museecanaldumidi.fr
www.odyssea.eu/oulibo/ (for the Olive Co-operative)
www.leparcaustralien.fr
www.parc-naturel-narbonnaise.fr
www.picarel-cerf.com
www.puilaurens.com
www.quercorb.com
www.rennes-le-chateau.fr
www.saintpapoul.fr
www.reserveafricainesigean.fr

Music Festivals

www.festivaldecarcassonne.fr
www.estivales.org   (for Organ concerts in the *Cité*)
www.festival-fontcalvy.com
www.fuguepassiclassique.fr
 www.jazz-roquefere.com
www.fontfroide.com

Outdoor Activities

http://aleteauvive.fr
www.aude-pyrenees.fr
www.espaceliberte.com
www.mellowvelos.com
www.mondial-du-vent.com
www.o2aventure.com
www.vtt-pyrenees.com
www.lesentiercathare.com
www.snkite.com

Wine

http://cabardes.free.fr
www.corbieresweb.com
www.chateaudelastours.com
www.chateaustjacques.com
www.la-clape.com
www.fitouaoc.com
www.languedoc-wines.com
www.lauran-cabaret.com
www.lechai-portminervois.com
www.leminervois.com
www.limoux-aoc.com
www.terra-vinea.fr
www.vins-malepere.com

The Coast

www.gruissan-mediterranee.com
www.tourisme-leucate.fr
www.narbonne.latitude-gallimard.com
www.narbonne-tourism.co.uk
www.portlanouvelle.com

Some Tourist Offices

www.aletlesbains.com
 www.tourisme-cabardes.fr
www.tourisme-carcassonne.fr
www.castelnaudary-tourisme.com
www.caunes-minervois.com
www.fitou.fr
www.lezignan-corbieres.fr/tourisme
www.limoux.fr
www.ot-mirepoix.fr
www.montreal-aude.fr
www.mairie-narbonne.fr
www.paysdecouiza.fr
www.renneslesbains.org
www.sallelesdaude.fr
www.villeneuve-minervois.com

Better a little French than none at all

bonjour	hello, good day
bonsoir	good evening
s'il vous plaît (svp)	please
merci	thank you
d'accord	OK
au revoir	goodbye
oui	yes
non	no

At a café/restaurant

je voudrais …	I would like …
une table pour deux personnes svp	a table for two, please
une bière svp	a beer please
pression	draught (beer)
un grand café crème	coffee with milk
un thé au lait svp	tea with milk please
une glace au chocolat	a chocolate ice
le menu fixe svp	the set menu, please
je prends le menu à vingt euros	I'll take the 20 euro menu
un pichet du vin rouge	a jug of the house red
qu'est-ce que c'est?	what's this?
je suis vegetarian	I am a vegetarian
qu'est ce que vous recommendez	what do you recommend?
c'est tout	that's all
l'addition, svp	the bill, please
c'est bon	that's fine
il y a une erreur	there's a mistake

Asking for directions

où est ….?	where is ….?
à gauche	on the left
à droite	on the right
tout droit	straight ahead
c'est loin?	Is it far?
où sont les toilettes?	where are the toilets?
où est l'office de tourisme?	where is the tourist office?

Some common signs

fermé	closed
ouvert	open
occupé	engaged
en panne	out of order
eau potable	drinking water
réservé aux riverains	residents' parking only
la navette	shuttle service

Other useful words and phrases

Avez-vous ?	do you have any?
je peux goûter?	may I taste some?
je voudrais louer…	I'd like to hire a…
pouvez vous m'aider	can you help?
à quelle heure est ?	at what time is ..?
au secours!	help!
aujourd'hui	today
demain	tomorrow
hier	yesterday
nous sommes en vacances	we are on holiday
nous sommes d'Angleterre/d'Irlande	We are from England/Ireland
désolé, je ne parle pas français	I'm sorry, I don't speak French
je ne comprends pas	I don't understand
parlez lentement svp	please speak slowly
parlez vous anglais?	do you speak English?
c'est combien?	how much is it?

Some road signs

autoroute	motorway
péage	toll plaza
sortie	exit
cédéz le passage	give way
ralentissez	slow down
route barrée	road closed
inondation	flooding